Introducing Go

Build Reliable, Scalable Programs

Caleb Doxsey

Beijing · Boston · Farnham · Sebastopol · Tokyo

Introducing Go

by Caleb Doxsey

Printed in the United States of America.

Published by O'Reilly Media, Inc., 1005 Gravenstein Highway North, Sebastopol, CA 95472.

O'Reilly books may be purchased for educational, business, or sales promotional use. Online editions are also available for most titles (*http://safaribooksonline.com*). For more information, contact our corporate/institutional sales department: 800-998-9938 or *corporate@oreilly.com*.

Editors: Brian MacDonald and Meghan Blanchette	**Indexer:** WordCo Indexing Services, Inc.
Production Editor: Shiny Kalapurakkel	**Interior Designer:** David Futato
Copyeditor: Jasmine Kwityn	**Cover Designer:** Karen Montgomery
Proofreader: James Fraleigh	**Illustrator:** Rebecca Demarest

January 2016:   First Edition

Revision History for the First Edition
2016-01-06:   First Release

See *http://oreilly.com/catalog/errata.csp?isbn=9781491941959* for release details.

978-1-491-94195-9

[LSI]

Table of Contents

Introduction

Although originally designed by Google for the kinds of problems Google works on —large, distributed network applications—Go is now a general-purpose programming language useful in a wide variety of software domains. Many companies have started using Go because of its simplicity, ease of use, performance, low barrier of entry, and powerful tooling.

This book was written to help new programmers learn Go. Although there is an abundance of technical resources available for Go, most are geared toward experienced engineers. My goal here is to provide a more gentle introduction to the language.

Who Should Read This Book

This book is written for relatively inexperienced programmers who know nothing about Go. Although not exhaustive, it does cover all of the basics, and should leave you well positioned to tackle the more advanced material available on the language. The book also covers rudimentary programming skills via the exercises at the end of each chapter.

Navigating This Book

This book is organized as follows:

- Chapters 1 through 4 introduce the Go toolset and the basics of the language
- Chapters 5 through 7 describe more complex types and functions
- Chapters 8 and 9 describe packages and testing
- Chapter 10 introduces concurrency

For best results, the book should be read in order, as each chapter builds on the concepts covered in the preceding chapters. Each chapter ends with a set of exercises, and it's important to actually complete them—it's by solving problems like these that you learn to program. In particular, typing out the examples (and not just reading them) can help significantly.

Online Resources

You'll want to check out the following resources:

- The Official Go Website (*http://www.golang.org*)
- The Go Tour (*http://tour.golang.org*)

Conventions Used in This Book

The following typographical conventions are used in this book:

Italic
> Indicates new terms, URLs, email addresses, filenames, and file extensions.

`Constant width`
> Used for program listings, as well as within paragraphs to refer to program elements such as variable or function names, databases, data types, environment variables, statements, and keywords.

`Constant width bold`
> Shows commands or other text that should be typed literally by the user.

`Constant width italic`
> Shows text that should be replaced with user-supplied values or by values determined by context.

Using Code Examples

This book is here to help you get your job done. In general, if example code is offered with this book, you may use it in your programs and documentation. You do not need to contact us for permission unless you're reproducing a significant portion of the code. For example, writing a program that uses several chunks of code from this book does not require permission. Selling or distributing a CD-ROM of examples from O'Reilly books does require permission. Answering a question by citing this book and quoting example code does not require permission. Incorporating a significant amount of example code from this book into your product's documentation does require permission.

We appreciate, but do not require, attribution. An attribution usually includes the title, author, publisher, and ISBN. For example: "*Introducing Go* by Caleb Doxsey (O'Reilly). Copyright 2016 Caleb Doxsey, 978-1-4919-4195-9."

If you feel your use of code examples falls outside fair use or the permission given above, feel free to contact us at *permissions@oreilly.com*.

Safari® Books Online

Safari Books Online is an on-demand digital library that delivers expert content in both book and video form from the world's leading authors in technology and business.

Technology professionals, software developers, web designers, and business and creative professionals use Safari Books Online as their primary resource for research, problem solving, learning, and certification training.

Safari Books Online offers a range of plans and pricing for enterprise, government, education, and individuals.

Members have access to thousands of books, training videos, and prepublication manuscripts in one fully searchable database from publishers like O'Reilly Media, Prentice Hall Professional, Addison-Wesley Professional, Microsoft Press, Sams, Que, Peachpit Press, Focal Press, Cisco Press, John Wiley & Sons, Syngress, Morgan Kaufmann, IBM Redbooks, Packt, Adobe Press, FT Press, Apress, Manning, New Riders, McGraw-Hill, Jones & Bartlett, Course Technology, and hundreds more. For more information about Safari Books Online, please visit us online.

How to Contact Us

Please address comments and questions concerning this book to the publisher:

O'Reilly Media, Inc.
1005 Gravenstein Highway North
Sebastopol, CA 95472
800-998-9938 (in the United States or Canada)
707-829-0515 (international or local)
707-829-0104 (fax)

We have a web page for this book, where we list errata, examples, and any additional information. You can access this page at bit.ly/introducing-go.

To comment or ask technical questions about this book, send email to *bookquestions@oreilly.com*.

For more information about our books, courses, conferences, and news, see our website at *http://www.oreilly.com*.

Find us on Facebook: *http://facebook.com/oreilly*

Follow us on Twitter: *http://twitter.com/oreillymedia*

Watch us on YouTube: *http://www.youtube.com/oreillymedia*

CHAPTER 1

Getting Started

Go is a general-purpose programming language with advanced features and a clean syntax. Because of its wide availability on a variety of platforms, its robust well-documented common library, and its focus on good software engineering principles, Go is a great programming language to learn.

This book assumes no prior knowledge of Go, and is intended to serve as an easy introduction to the language. All of the language's core features will be covered in short, concise chapters that should prepare you to write real Go programs and tackle some of the more advanced resources available on the language (online documentation, books, talks, etc.).

Although this book is suitable for inexperienced programmers, if you have never programmed before you will probably find the material too difficult to follow. You may benefit from consulting a more general programming resource before diving into the material here, but in all honesty, most students need the kind of hands-on, personal support that you might find in a classroom setting or one on one with an experienced developer.

Machine Setup

This book contains many code samples and exercises. For best results, you should try to run these examples on your own computer as you work your way through each chapter.

But before you can write your first Go program, there are a few things you will need to set up.

Text Editors

Go is a very readable, succinct language and so any text editor will work for editing files. There are plug-ins that add a few helpful features (like autocomplete and format-on-save) for many popular editors, but those plug-ins are not necessary to learn the language. If you're not sure what to use, I recommend using GitHub's Atom —it's free, cross-platform, and easy to install from the Atom website (*https://atom.io/*).

The Terminal

Go is a compiled language, and like many languages, it makes heavy use of the command line. If you're coming from a language that does most things through an IDE (such as Java or C#), this may be a bit intimidating, but thankfully, the Go tools are fairly easy to use. As a reminder, here's how you can get to a terminal:

Windows
On Windows, the terminal (also known as the command prompt) can be brought up by pressing the Windows key + R (hold down the Windows key, then press R), typing cmd.exe, and hitting Enter.

OS X
On OS X, the terminal can be reached by navigating to Finder → Applications → Utilities → Terminal.

Environment

Environment variables are a mechanism provided by your operating system for altering the behavior of a program without having to change it. An environment is a collection of these variables, each of which has a name and a corresponding value. For example, there is a TEMP environment variable that stores the location of a directory on your computer where temporary files are stored.

The Go toolset uses an environment variable called GOPATH to find Go source code. Although you're welcome to set the GOPATH to anything you want, to make things easier we will set it to be the same as your home directory:

Windows
On Windows, user information is typically stored in *C:\Users\<USERNAME>*, where *<USERNAME>* would be replaced with your username (e.g., *C:\Users \alice*). Windows comes with a predefined environment variable called USERPRO FILE, which you can use to set your GOPATH.

Open a new terminal window and enter the following:

```
setx GOPATH %USERPROFILE%
```

If you're using a version of Windows prior to Vista, this command may not work, so you can also set environment variables by navigating to Control Panel → System → Advanced → Environment Variables.

OS X

On OS X, user information is typically stored in */Users/<USERNAME>*, where *<USERNAME>* would be replaced with your username (e.g., /Users/alice). On OS X, we will set GOPATH using a special initialization file for the terminal called *.bash_profile*.

Open a terminal and enter the following:

```
echo 'export GOPATH=$HOME\n' >> ~/.bash_profile
```

Close the terminal, reopen it, and enter the following:

```
env
```

Among many other environment variables, you should see an entry for GOPATH.

Go

Go is both the name of the programming language and the name for the toolset used to build and interact with Go programs. Before you begin working with Go, you'll need to install the Go toolset.

Download and run the installer for your platform from *golang.org/dl*.

To confirm everything is working, open a terminal and type the following:

```
go version
```

You should see the following (your version number and operating system may be slightly different):

```
go version go1.5 windows/amd64
```

If you get an error about the command not being recognized, try restarting your computer.

The Go toolset is made up of several different commands and subcommands. You can pull up a list of those commands by typing:

```
go help
```

With Go installed and working, you now have everything you need to write your first Go program.

Your First Program

Traditionally, the first program you write in any programming language is called a "Hello, World" program—a program that simply outputs Hello, World to your terminal. Let's write one using Go.

First, create a new folder where you can store our "Hello, World" program. Create a folder named ~/src/golang-book/chapter1. From the terminal, you can do this by entering the following commands:

On Windows
```
md src\golang-book\chapter1
```

On OS X
```
mkdir -p src/golang-book/chapter1
```

Open your text editor, create a new file, and enter the following:

```
package main

import "fmt"

// this is a comment

func main() {
    fmt.Println("Hello, World")
}
```

Make sure your file is identical to what is shown here and save it as *main.go* in the folder we just created. Open up a new terminal and type in the following:

```
cd src/golang-book/chapter1
go run main.go
```

You should see Hello, World displayed in your terminal. The go run command takes the subsequent files (separated by spaces), compiles them into an executable saved in a temporary directory, and then runs the program. If you didn't see Hello, World displayed, you may have made a mistake when typing in the program. The Go compiler will give you hints about where the mistake lies. Like most compilers, the Go compiler is extremely pedantic and has no tolerance for mistakes.

How to Read a Go Program

Let's look at this program in more detail:

```go
package main

import "fmt"

// this is a comment

func main() {
    fmt.Println("Hello, World")
}
```

Go programs are read top to bottom, left to right (like a book). The first line says this:

```go
package main
```

This is known as a *package declaration*, and every Go program must start with it. Packages are Go's way of organizing and reusing code. There are two types of Go programs: executables and libraries. Executable applications are the kinds of programs that we can run directly from the terminal (on Windows, they end with *.exe*). Libraries are collections of code that we package together so that we can use them in other programs. We will explore libraries in more detail later; for now, just make sure to include this line in any program you write.

The next line is blank. Computers represent newlines with a special character (or several characters). Newlines, spaces, and tabs are known as whitespace (because you can't see them). Go mostly doesn't care about whitespace—we use it to make programs easier to read (you could remove this line and the program would behave in exactly the same way).

On the following line, we see this:

```go
import "fmt"
```

The import keyword is how we include code from other packages to use with our program. The fmt package (shorthand for format) implements formatting for input and output. Given what we just learned about packages, what do you think the fmt package's files would contain at the top of them?[1]

Notice that fmt is surrounded by double quotes. The use of double quotes like this is known as a *string literal*, which is a type of *expression*. In Go, strings represent a sequence of characters (letters, numbers, symbols, etc.) of a definite length. Strings are described in more detail in the next chapter, but for now the important thing to

---

1 Files in the fmt package start with package fmt.

keep in mind is that an opening " character must eventually be followed by a closing " character and anything in between the two is included in the string (the " character itself is not part of the string).

The line that starts with // is known as a *comment*. Comments are ignored by the Go compiler and are there for your own sake (or whoever picks up the source code for your program). Go supports two different styles of comments: // comments in which all the text between the // and the end of the line is part of the comment, and /* */ comments where everything between the asterisks is part of the comment (and may include multiple lines).

After this, you see a function declaration:

```
func main() {
    fmt.Println("Hello, World")
}
```

Functions are the building blocks of a Go program. They have inputs, outputs, and a series of steps called statements that are executed in order. All functions start with the keyword func followed by the name of the function (main, in this case), a list of zero or more *parameters* surrounded by parentheses, an optional return type, and a *body* which is surrounded by curly braces. This function has no parameters, doesn't return anything, and has only one statement. The name main is special because it's the function that gets called when you execute the program.

The final piece of our program is this line:

```
fmt.Println("Hello, World")
```

This statement is made of three components. First, we access another function inside of the fmt package called Println (that's the fmt.Println piece); Println means "print line." Then we create a new string that contains Hello, World and *invoke* (also known as *call* or *execute*) that function with the string as the first and only argument.

At this point, you've already seen a lot of new terminology. Sometimes it's helpful to deliberately read your program out loud. One reading of the program we just wrote might go like this:

> Create a new executable program that references the fmt library and contains one function called main. That function takes no arguments and doesn't return anything. It accesses the Println function contained inside of the fmt package and invokes it using one argument—the string Hello, World.

The Println function does the real work in this program. You can find out more about it by typing the following in your terminal:

```
godoc fmt Println
```

Among other things, you should see the output shown in Figure 1-1.

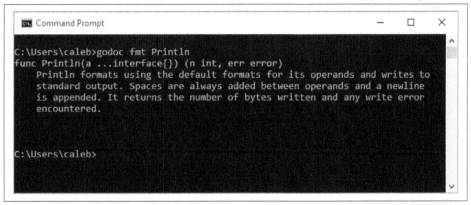

Figure 1-1. Output of godoc fmt Println

Println formats using the default formats for its operands and writes to standard output. Spaces are always added between operands and a newline is appended. It returns the number of bytes written and any write error encountered.

Go is a very well-documented programming language, but this documentation can be difficult to understand unless you are already familiar with programming languages. Nevertheless, the godoc command is extremely useful and a good place to start whenever you have a question.

Back to the function at hand, this documentation is telling you that the Println function will send whatever you give to it to *standard output* (i.e., the output of the terminal you are working in). This function is what causes Hello, World to be displayed.

In the next chapter, we will explore how Go stores and represents things like Hello, World by learning about types.

Exercises

1. What is whitespace?
2. What is a comment? What are the two ways of writing a comment?
3. Our program began with package main. What would the files in the fmt package begin with?
4. We used the Println function defined in the fmt package. If you wanted to use the Exit function from the os package, what would you need to do?
5. Modify the program we wrote so that instead of printing Hello, World it prints Hello, my name is followed by your name.

Types

In the previous chapter, we used the data type string to store Hello, World. Data types categorize a set of related values, describe the operations that can be done on them, and define the way they are stored. Because types can be a difficult concept to grasp, we will look at them from a couple different perspectives before we see how they are implemented in Go.

Philosophers sometimes make a distinction between types and tokens. For example, suppose you have a dog named Max. *Max* is the token (a particular instance or member) and *dog* is the type (the general concept). *Dog* or *dogness* describes a set of properties that all dogs have in common. Although oversimplistic, we might reason like this: all dogs have four legs, Max is a dog, therefore Max has four legs. Types in programming languages work in a similar way: all strings have a length, *x* is a string, therefore *x* has a length.

In mathematics, we often talk about sets. For example, $\mathbb{R}$ (the set of all real numbers) or $\mathbb{N}$ (the set of all natural numbers). Each member of these sets shares properties with all the other members of the set. For instance, all natural numbers are associative: "for all natural numbers a, b, and c, $a + (b + c) = (a + b) + c$ and $a \times (b \times c) = (a \times b) \times c$." In this way, sets are similar to types in programming languages, because all the values of a particular type share certain properties.

Go is a statically typed programming language. This means that variables always have a specific type and that type cannot change. Static typing may seem cumbersome at first. You'll spend a large amount of your time just trying to fix your program so that it finally compiles. But types help us reason about what our program is doing and catch a wide variety of common mistakes.

Go comes with several built-in data types, which we will now look at in more detail.

Numbers

Go has several different types to represent numbers. Generally, we split numbers into two different kinds: integers and floating-point numbers.

Integers

Integers—like their mathematical counterpart—are numbers without a decimal component. (…, −3, −2, −1, 0, 1, …) Unlike the base-10 decimal system we use to represent numbers, computers use a base-2 binary system.

Our system is made up of 10 different digits. Once we've exhausted our available digits, we represent larger numbers by using 2 (then 3, 4, 5, etc.) digits put next to each other. For example, the number after 9 is 10, the number after 99 is 100, and so on. Computers do the same, but they only have 2 digits instead of 10. So counting looks like this: 0, 1, 10, 11, 100, 101, 110, 111, and so on. The other difference between the number system we use and the one computers use is that all of the integer types have a definite size. They only have room for a certain number of digits. So a 4-bit integer might look like this: 0000, 0001, 0010, 0011, 0100. Eventually we run out of space and most computers just wrap around to the beginning (which can result in some very strange behavior).

Go's integer types are uint8, uint16, uint32, uint64, int8, int16, int32, and int64. 8, 16, 32, and 64 tell us how many bits each of the types use. uint means "unsigned integer" while int means "signed integer." Unsigned integers only contain positive numbers (or zero). In addition, there two alias types: byte (which is the same as uint8) and rune (which is the same as int32). Bytes are an extremely common unit of measurement used on computers (1 byte = 8 bits, 1,024 bytes = 1 kilobyte, 1,024 kilobytes = 1 megabyte, etc.) and therefore Go's byte data type is often used in the definition of other types. There are also three machine dependent integer types: uint, int, and uintptr. They are machine dependent because their size depends on the type of architecture you are using.

Generally, if you are working with integers, you should just use the int type.

Floating-Point Numbers

Floating-point numbers are numbers that contain a decimal component (i.e., real numbers). For example, 1.234, 123.4, 0.00001234, and 12340000 are all floating-point numbers. Their actual representation on a computer is fairly complicated and it's not really necessary to know the particulars in order to use them. So, for now, you only need to keep the following in mind:

- Floating-point numbers are inexact. Occasionally it is not possible to represent a number. For example, computing 1.01 – 0.99 using floating-point arithmetic results in 0.020000000000000018—a number extremely close to what we would expect, but not exactly the same.
- Like integers, floating-point numbers have a certain size (32 bit or 64 bit). Using a larger-sized floating-point number increases its precision (i.e., how many digits it can represent).
- In addition to numbers, there are several other values that can be represented: "not a number" (NaN, for things like 0/0) and positive and negative infinity (+∞ and –∞).

Go has two floating-point types: float32 and float64 (also often referred to as single precision and double precision, respectively). It also has two additional types for representing complex numbers (numbers with imaginary parts): complex64 and complex128. Generally, we should stick with float64 when working with floating-point numbers.

Example

Let's write an example program using numbers. First, create a folder called *chapter2* and make a *main.go* file containing the following:

```
package main

import "fmt"

func main() {
    fmt.Println("1 + 1 =", 1 + 1)
}
```

If you run the program, you should see this:

```
$ go run main.go
1 + 1 = 2
```

Notice that this program is very similar to the program we wrote in Chapter 1. It contains the same package line, the same import line, and the same function declaration, and it uses the same Println function. However, instead of printing the string Hello, World, we print the string 1 + 1 = followed by the result of the expression 1 + 1. This expression is made up of three parts: the numeric literal 1 (which is of type int), the + operator (which represents addition), and another numeric literal 1. Let's try the same thing using floating-point numbers:

```
fmt.Println("1 + 1 =", 1.0 + 1.0)
```

Notice that we use the .0 to tell Go that this is a floating-point number instead of an integer. Running this program will give you the same result as before.

Go supports the following standard arithmetic operators:

+

Addition

-

Subtraction

*

Multiplication

/

Division

%

Remainder

This small set of basic operators, along with some of the helper functions available in the math package, is sufficient to create surprisingly sophisticated programs. Another type we use in almost every Go program is a *string*.

Strings

As we saw in Chapter 1, a string is a sequence of characters with a definite length used to represent text. Go strings are made up of individual bytes, usually one for each character (characters from some languages, such as Chinese, are represented by more than one byte).

String literals can be created using double quotes "Hello, World" or backticks `Hello, World`. The difference between these is that double-quoted strings cannot contain newlines and they allow special escape sequences. For example, \n gets replaced with a newline and \t gets replaced with a tab character.

The following are some common operations on strings:

len("Hello, World")
    Finds the length of a string

"Hello, World"[1]
    Accesses a particular character in the string (in this case, the second character)

"Hello, " + World"
    Concatenates two strings together

Let's modify the program we created earlier to test these out:

```go
package main

import "fmt"

func main() {
    fmt.Println(len("Hello, World"))
    fmt.Println("Hello, World"[1])
    fmt.Println("Hello, " + "World")
}
```

A few things to notice:

- A space is also considered a character, so the string's length is 12, not 11, and the third line has "Hello, " instead of "Hello".
- Strings are *indexed* starting at 0, not 1. [1] gives you the second element, not the first. Also notice that you see 101 instead of e when you run this program. This is because the character is represented by a byte (remember a byte is an integer).

  One way to think about indexing would be to show it like this instead: "Hello, World"$_1$. You'd read that as "The string Hello, World sub 1," "The string Hello, World at 1," or "The second character of the string Hello, World."

- Concatenation uses the same symbol as addition. The Go compiler figures out what to do based on the types of the arguments. Because both sides of the + are strings, the compiler assumes you mean concatenation and not addition (addition is meaningless for strings).

Strings and numbers are both extremely useful. Most programs either represent mathematical formulas or involve the manipulation and transformation of data, which is usually represented as a string (or a byte slice, as we will see later). But there's a third basic type that is needed by almost any program, and that's a *boolean*.

Booleans

A boolean value (named after George Boole) is a special 1-bit integer type used to represent true and false (or on and off). Three logical operators are used with boolean values:

&&   and

|| or

!   not

Here is an example program showing how they can be used:

```
func main() {
    fmt.Println(true && true)
    fmt.Println(true && false)
    fmt.Println(true || true)
    fmt.Println(true || false)
    fmt.Println(!true)
}
```

Running this program should give you:

```
$ go run main.go
true
false
true
true
false
```

We usually use truth tables to define how these operators work:

Expression	Value
true && true	true
true && false	false
false && true	false
false && false	false

Expression	Value
true || true	true
true || false	true
false || true	true
false || false	false

Expression	Value
!true	false
!false	true

We often use booleans to make decisions in our program and represent binary distinctions (Has a feature been enabled? Is this user an administrator? Have I found the value I was looking for?). As you see more examples and write more code, you will gain a better understanding of how and when to use them.

These are the simplest types included with Go, and they form the foundation from which all later types are built. In the next chapter, we will see how these types can be used to store data in your program with variables.

Exercises

1. How are integers stored on a computer?
2. We know that (in base 10) the largest one-digit number is 9 and the largest two-digit number is 99. Given that in binary the largest two-digit number is 11 (3), the largest three-digit number is 111 (7) and the largest four-digit number is 1111 (15), what's the largest eight-digit number? (Hint: $10^1-1 = 9$ and $10^2-1 = 99$) $2^8-1 = 255$
3. Although overpowered for the task, you can use Go as a calculator. Write a program that computes $32,132 \times 42,452$ and prints it to the terminal (use the * operator for multiplication).
4. What is a string? How do you find its length?
5. What's the value of the expression (true && false) || (false && true) || ! (false && false)?

Variables

Up until now, we have only seen programs that use literal values (numbers, strings, etc.), but such programs aren't particularly useful. To make truly useful programs, we need to discuss two new concepts: variables and control flow statements. This chapter will explore variables in more detail (we'll discuss control flow statements in Chapter 4).

A variable is a storage location, with a specific type and an associated name. Let's change the program we wrote in Chapter 1 so that it uses a variable:

```
package main

import "fmt"

func main() {
    var x string = "Hello, World"
    fmt.Println(x)
}
```

Notice that the string literal from the original program still appears in this program, but rather than send it directly to the Println function, we assign it to a variable instead. Variables in Go are created by first using the var keyword, then specifying the variable name (x) and the type (string), and finally, assigning a value to the variable (Hello, World). Assigning a value is optional, so we could use two statements, like this:

```
package main

import "fmt"

func main() {
    var x string
    x = "Hello, World"
```

```
        fmt.Println(x)
    }
```

Variables in Go are similar to variables in algebra, but there are some subtle differences. First, when we see the = symbol, we have a tendency to read that as "x equals the string Hello, World." There's nothing wrong with reading our program that way, but it's better to read it as "x takes the string Hello, World" or "x is assigned the string Hello, World." This distinction is important because (as their name would suggest) variables can change their value throughout the lifetime of a program. Try running the following:

```
package main

import "fmt"

func main() {
    var x string
    x = "first"
    fmt.Println(x)
    x = "second"
    fmt.Println(x)
}
```

In fact, you can even do this:

```
var x string
x = "first "
fmt.Println(x)
x = x + "second"
fmt.Println(x)
```

This program would be nonsense if you read it like an algebraic theorem. But it makes sense if you are careful to read the program as a list of commands. When we see x = x + "second", we should read it as "assign the concatenation of the value of the variable x and the string literal second to the variable x." The right side of the = is done first and the result is then assigned to the left side of the =.

The x = x + y form is so common in programming that Go has a special assignment statement: +=. We could have written x = x + "second" as x += "second" and it would have done the same thing (other operators can be used the same way).

Another difference between Go and algebra is that we use a different symbol for equality: == (two equals signs next to each other). == is an operator like + and it returns a boolean. For example:

```
var x string = "hello"
var y string = "world"
fmt.Println(x == y)
```

This program should print `false` because `hello` is not the same as `world`. On the other hand:

```
var x string = "hello"
var y string = "hello"
fmt.Println(x == y)
```

This will print `true` because the two strings are the same.

Because creating a new variable with a starting value is so common, Go also supports a shorter statement:

```
x := "Hello, World"
```

Notice the : before the = and that no type was specified. The type is not necessary because the Go compiler is able to infer the type based on the literal value you assign the variable (because you are assigning a string literal, x is given the type `string`). The compiler can also do inference with the `var` statement:

```
var x = "Hello, World"
```

The same thing works for other types:

```
x := 5
fmt.Println(x)
```

Generally, you should use this shorter form whenever possible.

Idiomatic Go

Languages often have a set of informal, conventional rules. For example, in English, there are rules that govern the order of adjectives in a sentence. If, instead of "my small black cat," you were to say, "my black small cat," it would strike native speakers as very strange.

Programming languages often exhibit the same phenomenon. Although there are often many ways to do something, not all of those ways are seen as a natural expression of the language. You may write an expression (var x int = 5) which is semantically valid in the language (it compiles), but which may look strange to experienced Go programmers.

Go programmers (as well as programmers in other communities) often refer to this as the idiomatic usage of the language. Learning idiomatic Go is a worthwhile pursuit, but at this stage, you should probably focus on simply writing correct programs, as that's challenging enough. Don't let the best be the enemy of the good.

How to Name a Variable

Naming a variable properly is an important part of software development. Names must start with a letter and may contain letters, numbers, or the underscore symbol (_). The Go compiler doesn't care what you name a variable, but you should choose names that clearly describe the variable's purpose. Suppose we had the following:

```
x := "Max"
fmt.Println("My dog's name is", x)
```

In this case, x is not a very good name for a variable. A better name would be:

```
name := "Max"
fmt.Println("My dog's name is", name)
```

or even:

```
dogsName := "Max"
fmt.Println("My dog's name is", dogsName)
```

In the preceding snippet, we use camelCase, which is a style for writing compound words in which the first letter of each new word or phrase is capitalized. It is also sometimes referred to as mixedCase, BumpyCaps, camelBack, or HumpBack (in some other languages, the first letter is also capitalized).

Scope

Let's take another look at the program we saw at the beginning of the chapter:

```
package main

import "fmt"

func main() {
    var x string = "Hello, World"
    fmt.Println(x)
}
```

Another way of writing this program would be like this:

```
package main

import "fmt"

var x string = "Hello, World"

func main() {
    fmt.Println(x)
}
```

Notice that we moved the variable outside of the main function. This means that other functions can access this variable:

```
var x string = "Hello, World"

func main() {
    fmt.Println(x)
}

func f() {
    fmt.Println(x)
}
```

The f function now has access to the x variable. Now suppose that we wrote this instead:

```
func main() {
    var x string = "Hello, World"
    fmt.Println(x)
}

func f() {
    fmt.Println(x)
}
```

If you run this program, you should see an error:

```
.\main.go:11: undefined: x
```

The compiler is telling you that the x variable inside of the f function doesn't exist. It only exists inside of the main function. The range of places where you are allowed to use x is called the scope of the variable. According to the language specification, "Go is lexically scoped using blocks." Basically, this means that the variable exists within the nearest curly braces ({ }), or block, including any nested curly braces (blocks), but not outside of them. Scope can be a little confusing at first; as we see more Go examples, it should become more clear.

Constants

Go also has support for constants. Constants are essentially variables whose values cannot be changed later. They are created in the same way you create variables, but instead of using the var keyword we use the const keyword:

```
package main

import "fmt"

func main() {
    const x string = "Hello, World"
    fmt.Println(x)
}
```

This:

```
const x string = "Hello, World"
x = "Some other string"
```

Results in a compile-time error:

```
.\main.go:7: cannot assign to x
```

Constants are a good way to reuse common values in a program without writing them out each time. For example, Pi in the math package is defined as a constant.

Defining Multiple Variables

Go also has another shorthand when you need to define multiple variables:

```
var (
    a = 5
    b = 10
    c = 15
)
```

[handwritten: also :, const (
var₁,
var₂
...
)]

[handwritten margin mark: ✗]

Use the keyword var (or const) followed by parentheses with each variable on its own line.

An Example Program

Here's an example program that takes in a number entered by the user and doubles it:

```
package main

import "fmt"

func main() {
    fmt.Print("Enter a number: ")        // No new line
    var input float64
    fmt.Scanf("%f", &input)

    output := input * 2

    fmt.Println(output)
}
```

[handwritten: // No new line]

We use another function from the fmt package to read the user input (Scanf). &input will be explained in a later chapter; for now, all you need to know is that Scanf fills input with the number we enter.

Exercises

1. What are two ways to create a new variable?
2. What is the value of x after running x := 5; x += 1?
3. What is scope? How do you determine the scope of a variable in Go?
4. What is the difference between var and const?
5. Using the example program as a starting point, write a program that converts from Fahrenheit into Celsius (C = (F − 32) * 5/9).
6. Write another program that converts from feet into meters (1 ft = 0.3048 m).

5.

```
package main
import "fmt"

func main() {
    fmt.Print("Enter a temperature value in Fahrenheit: ")
    var fahrenheit float64
    var celsius   float64
    fmt.Scanf("%f", &fahrenheit)
    celsius = (fahrenheit - 32.0) * 5.0/9.0
    fmt.Print("Temperature:", fahrenheit, "in fahrenheit is:",
              celsius, "in celsus")
}
```

CHAPTER 4

Control Structures

Now that you know how to use variables, it's time to start writing some useful programs. First, let's write a program that counts to 10, starting from 1, with each number on its own line. Using what you've learned so far, you could write this:

```
package main

import "fmt"

func main() {
    fmt.Println(1)
    fmt.Println(2)
    fmt.Println(3)
    fmt.Println(4)
    fmt.Println(5)
    fmt.Println(6)
    fmt.Println(7)
    fmt.Println(8)
    fmt.Println(9)
    fmt.Println(10)
}
```

Or this:

```
package main
import "fmt"

func main() {
  fmt.Println(`1
2
3
4
5
6
7
```

```
8
9
10`)
}
```

But both of these programs are pretty tedious to write. What we need is a way of doing something multiple times.

The for Statement

The `for` statement allows us to repeat a list of statements (a block) multiple times. Rewriting our previous program using a `for` statement looks like this:

```
package main

import "fmt"

func main() {
    i := 1
    for i <= 10 {
        fmt.Println(i)
        i = i + 1
    }
}
```

First, we create a variable called i that we use to store the number we want to print. Then we create a for loop by using the keyword for, providing a conditional expression that is either true or false and finally supplying a block to execute. The for loop works like this:

1. We evaluate (run) the expression i <= 10 ("i less than or equal to 10"). If this evaluates to true, then we run the statements inside of the block. Otherwise, we jump to the next line of our program after the block (in this case, there is nothing after the for loop, so we exit the program).

2. After we run the statements inside of the block, we loop back to the beginning of the for statement and repeat step 1.

The i = i + 1 line is extremely important, because without it, i <= 10 would always evaluate to true and our program would never stop (when this happens, it's referred to as an infinite loop).

As an exercise, let's walk through the program like a computer would:

1. Create a variable named i with the value 1.

2. Is i <= 10? Yes.

3. Print i.

---

4. Set i to i + 1 (i now equals 2).

5. Is i <= 10? Yes.

6. Print i.

7. Set i to i + 1 (i now equals 3).

8. ...

9. Set i to i + 1 (i now equals 11).

10. Is i <= 10? No.

11. Nothing left to do, so exit.

Other programming languages have a lot of different types of loops (while, do, until, foreach, ...) but Go only has one that can be used in a variety of different ways. The previous program could also have been written like this:

```go
func main() {
    for i := 1; i <= 10; i++ {
        fmt.Println(i)
    }
}
```

Now the conditional expression also contains two other statements with semicolons between them. First, we have the variable initialization, then we have the condition to check each time, and finally, we *increment* the variable. Adding 1 to a variable is so common that we have a special operator (++); similarly, subtracting 1 can be done with --.

We will see additional ways of using the for loop in later chapters.

The if Statement

Let's modify the program we just wrote so that instead of just printing the numbers 1–10 on each line, it also specifies whether or not the number is even or odd:

```
1 odd
2 even
3 odd
4 even
5 odd
6 even
7 odd
8 even
9 odd
10 even
```

First, we need a way of determining whether or not a number is even or odd. An easy way to tell is to divide the number by 2. If you have nothing left over, then the number is even; otherwise, it's odd. So how do we find the remainder after division in Go? We use the % operator. 1 % 2 equals 1, 2 % 2 equals 0, 3 % 2 equals 1, and so on.

Next, we need a way of choosing to do different things based on a condition. For that, we use the if statement:

```
if i % 2 == 0 {
    // even
} else {
    // odd
}
```

An if statement is similar to a for statement in that it has a condition followed by a block. if statements also have an optional else part. If the condition evaluates to true, then the block after the condition is run; otherwise, either the block is skipped, or if the else block is present, that block is run.

if statements can also have else if parts:

```
if i % 2 == 0 {
    // divisible by 2
} else if i % 3 == 0 {
    // divisible by 3
} else if i % 4 == 0 {
    // divisible by 4
}
```

The conditions are checked top down and the first one to result in true will have its associated block executed. None of the other blocks will execute, even if their conditions also pass (so, for example, the number 8 is divisible by both 4 and 2, but the // divisible by 4 block will never execute because the // divisible by 2 block is done first).

Putting it all together, we have:

```
func main() {
    for i := 1; i <= 10; i++ {
        if i % 2 == 0 {
            fmt.Println(i, "even")
        } else {
            fmt.Println(i, "odd")
        }
    }
}
```

Let's walk through this program:

1. Create a variable i of type int and give it the value 1.
2. Is i less than or equal to 10? Yes: jump to the if block.
3. Is the remainder of i ÷ 2 equal to 0? No: jump to the else block.
4. Print i followed by odd.
5. Increment i (the statement after the condition).
6. Is i less than or equal to 10? Yes: jump to the if block.
7. Is the remainder of i ÷ 2 equal to 0? Yes: jump to the if block.
8. Print i followed by even, and so on until i is equal to 11.
9. …

The remainder operator, while rarely seen outside of elementary school, turns out to be really useful when programming. You'll see it turn up everywhere from zebra striping tables to partitioning data sets.

if statements are quite useful, but they can occasionally be quite verbose, so Go includes a related statement: the switch.

The switch Statement

Suppose you wanted to write a program that printed the English names for numbers. Using what you've learned so far, you might start by doing this:

```
if i == 0 {
    fmt.Println("Zero")
} else if i == 1 {
    fmt.Println("One")
} else if i == 2 {
    fmt.Println("Two")
} else if i == 3 {
    fmt.Println("Three")
} else if i == 4 {
    fmt.Println("Four")
} else if i == 5 {
    fmt.Println("Five")
}
```

Writing a program in this way would be pretty tedious, so another way of achieving the same result is to use the switch statement. We can rewrite our program to look like this:

```
switch i {
case 0: fmt.Println("Zero")
case 1: fmt.Println("One")
case 2: fmt.Println("Two")
case 3: fmt.Println("Three")
case 4: fmt.Println("Four")
case 5: fmt.Println("Five")
default: fmt.Println("Unknown Number")
}
```

A switch statement starts with the keyword switch followed by an expression (in this case, i) and then a series of cases. The value of the expression is compared to the expression following each case keyword. If they are equivalent, then the statements following the : are executed.

Like an if statement, each case is checked top down and the first one to succeed is chosen. A switch also supports a default case that will happen if none of the cases matches the value (similar to how the else works in an if statement).

for, if, and switch are the main control flow statements. Additional statements will be explored in later chapters.

Exercises

1. What does the following program print?

```
i := 10
if i > 10 {
    fmt.Println("Big")
} else {
    fmt.Println("Small")
}
```

2. Write a program that prints out all the numbers between 1 and 100 that are evenly divisible by 3 (i.e., 3, 6, 9, etc.).

3. Write a program that prints the numbers from 1 to 100, but for multiples of three, print "Fizz" instead of the number, and for the multiples of five, print "Buzz." For numbers that are multiples of both three and five, print "FizzBuzz."

CHAPTER 5

Arrays, Slices, and Maps

In Chapter 2, we learned about Go's basic types. In this chapter, we will look at three more built-in types: arrays, slices, and maps.

Arrays

An array is a numbered sequence of elements of a single type with a fixed length. In Go, they look like this:

```
var x [5]int
```

x is an example of an array that is composed of five ints. Try running the following program:

```
package main

import "fmt"

func main() {
    var x [5]int
    x[4] = 100
    fmt.Println(x)
}
```

You should see this:

```
[0 0 0 0 100]
```

x[4] = 100 should be read "set the fifth element of the array x to 100." It might seem strange that x[4] represents the fifth element instead of the fourth, but like strings, arrays are indexed starting from 0. Arrays are accessed in a similar way. We could change fmt.Println(x) to fmt.Println(x[4]) and we would get 100.

Here's an example program that uses arrays:

```go
func main() {
    var x [5]float64
    x[0] = 98
    x[1] = 93
    x[2] = 77
    x[3] = 82
    x[4] = 83

    var total float64 = 0
    for i := 0; i < 5; i++ {
        total += x[i]
    }
    fmt.Println(total / 5)
}
```

This program computes the average of a series of test scores. If you run it, you should see 86.6. Let's walk through the program:

1. First, we create an array of length 5 to hold our test scores, then we fill up each element with a grade.
2. Next, we set up a for loop to compute the total score.
3. Finally, we divide the total score by the number of elements to find the average.

This program works, but Go provides some features we can use to improve it. Specifically, i < 5 and total / 5 should throw up a red flag for us. Say we changed the number of grades from 5 to 6. We would also need to change both of these parts. It would be better to use the length of the array instead:

```go
var total float64 = 0
for i := 0; i < len(x); i++ {
    total += x[i]
}
fmt.Println(total / len(x))        // err
```

Go ahead and make these changes and run the program. You should get an error:

```
$ go run tmp.go
# command-line arguments
.\tmp.go:19: invalid operation: total / 5 (mismatched types float64 and int)
```

The issue here is that len(x) and total have different types. total is a float64 while len(x) is an int. So we need to convert len(x) into a float64:

```go
fmt.Println(total / float64(len(x)))
```

This is an example of a type conversion. In general, to convert between types, you use the type name like a function.

Another change to the program we can make is to use a special form of the for loop:

```
var total float64 = 0
for i, value := range x {        // var x [5] float64
    total += value
}
fmt.Println(total / float64(len(x)))
```

In this for loop, i represents the current position in the array and value is the same as x[i]. We use the keyword range followed by the name of the variable we want to loop over.

Running this program will result in another error:

```
$ go run tmp.go
# command-line arguments
.\tmp.go:16: i declared and not used
```

The Go compiler won't allow you to create variables that you never use. Because we don't use i inside of our loop, we need to change it to this:

```
var total float64 = 0
for _, value := range x {
    total += value
}
fmt.Println(total / float64(len(x)))
```

A single underscore (_) is used to tell the compiler that we don't need this (in this case, we don't need the iterator variable).

Go also provides a shorter syntax for creating arrays:

```
x := [5]float64{ 98, 93, 77, 82, 83 }
```

We no longer need to specify the type because Go can figure it out. Sometimes arrays like this can get too long to fit on one line, so Go allows you to break it up like this:

```
x := [5]float64{
    98,
    93,
    77,
    82,
    83,        // comma req'd by Go
}
```

Notice the extra trailing , after 83. This is required by Go and it allows us to easily remove an element from the array by commenting out the line:

```
x := [4]float64{
    98,
    93,
    77,
    82,
    // 83,
}
```

Because the length of an array is part of its type name, working with arrays can be a little cumbersome. Adding or removing elements as we did here requires also changing the length inside the brackets. Because of this and other limitations, you rarely see arrays used directly in Go code. Instead, you will usually use a *slice*, which is a type built on top of an array.

Slices

A slice is a segment of an array. Like arrays, slices are indexable and have a length. Unlike arrays, this length is allowed to change. Here's an example of a slice:

```
var x []float64
```

The only difference between this and an array is the missing length between the brackets. In this case, x has been created with a length of zero.

If you want to create a slice, you should use the built-in make function:

```
x := make([]float64, 5)
```

This creates a slice that is associated with an underlying float64 array of length 5. Slices are always associated with some array, and although they can never be longer than the array, they can be smaller. The make function also allows a third parameter:

```
x := make([]float64, 5, 10)
```

As illustrated in Figure 5-1, 10 represents the capacity of the underlying array that the slice points to:

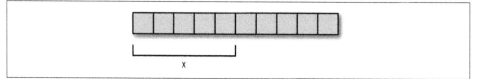

Figure 5-1. A slice of length 5 with a capacity of 10

Another way to create slices is to use the [low : high] expression:

```
arr := [5]float64{1,2,3,4,5}
x := arr[0:5]
```

low is the index of where to start the slice and high is the index of where to end it (but not including the index itself). For example, while arr[0:5] returns [1,2,3,4,5], arr[1:4] returns [2,3,4].

For convenience, we are also allowed to omit low, high, or even both low and high. arr[0:] is the same as arr[0:len(arr)], arr[:5] is the same as arr[0:5], and arr[:] is the same as arr[0:len(arr)].

In addition to the indexing operator, Go includes two built-in functions to assist with slices: append and copy.

append

append adds elements onto the end of a slice. If there's sufficient capacity in the underlying array, the element is placed after the last element and the length is incremented. However, if there is not sufficient capacity, a new array is created, all of the existing elements are copied over, the new element is added onto the end, and the new slice is returned.

The definition of append can be a bit confusing but it's easier to grasp once you see it used. Here is an example:

```
func main() {
    slice1 := []int{1,2,3}
    slice2 := append(slice1, 4, 5)
    fmt.Println(slice1, slice2)
}
```

After running this program, slice1 has [1,2,3] and slice2 has [1,2,3,4,5]. append creates a new slice by taking an existing slice (the first argument) and appending all the following arguments to it.

copy

copy takes two arguments: dst and src. All of the entries in src are copied into dst overwriting whatever is there. If the lengths of the two slices are not the same, the smaller of the two will be used.

Here is an example of copy:

```
func main() {
    slice1 := []int{1,2,3}
    slice2 := make([]int, 2)
    copy(slice2, slice1)              // copy (dst Slice, src Slice)      )
    fmt.Println(slice1, slice2)
}
```

After running this program slice1 has [1,2,3] and slice2 has [1,2]. The contents of slice1 are copied into slice2, but because slice2 has room for only two elements, only the first two elements of slice1 are copied.

Slices are typically used to represent lists of items, particularly when you need to access the *n*th item quickly—for example, player #33, or the 10th most popular search query. But what if you want to look up an entry by something other than integer? What if you wanted to look up a player on a team by last name? Go has another built-in type that can do this: a *map*.

Maps

A *map* is an unordered collection of key-value pairs (maps are also sometimes called associative arrays, hash tables, or dictionaries). Maps are used to look up a value by its associated key. Here's an example of a map in Go:

```
var x map[string]int
```

The map type is represented by the keyword map, followed by the key type in brackets and finally the value type. If you were to read this out loud, you would say "x is a map of strings to ints."

Like arrays and slices, maps can be accessed using brackets. Try running the following program:

```
var x map[string]int
x["key"] = 10
fmt.Println(x)
```

You should see an error similar to this:

```
panic: runtime error: assignment to entry in nil map

goroutine 1 [running]:
main.main()
main.go:7 +0x4d

goroutine 2 [syscall]:
created by runtime.main
    C:/Users/ADMINI~1/AppData/Local/Temp/2/bindi
t269497170/src/pkg/runtime/proc.c:221
exit status 2
```

Up until now, we have only seen compile-time errors. This is an example of a runtime error. As the name would imply, runtime errors happen when you run the program, while compile-time errors happen when you try to compile the program.

The problem with our program is that maps have to be initialized before they can be used. We should have written this:

```
x := make(map[string]int)
x["key"] = 10
fmt.Println(x["key"])
```

If you run this program, you should see 10 displayed. The statement x["key"] = 10 is similar to what we saw with arrays; however, instead of being an integer, the key is a string because the map's key type is string. We can also create maps with a key type of int:

```
x := make(map[int]int)
x[1] = 10
fmt.Println(x[1])
```

This looks very much like an array, but there are a few differences. First, the length of a map (found by doing `len(x)`) can change as we add new items to it. When initially created, it has a length of 0; after `x[1] = 10` it has a length of 1. Second, maps are not sequential. We have `x[1]`, and with an array that would imply there must be an `x[0]`, but maps don't have this requirement.

We can also delete items from a map using the built-in `delete` function:

```
delete(x, 1)
```

Let's look at an example program that uses a map:

```go
package main

import "fmt"

func main() {
    elements := make(map[string]string)
    elements["H"] = "Hydrogen"
    elements["He"] = "Helium"
    elements["Li"] = "Lithium"
    elements["Be"] = "Beryllium"
    elements["B"] = "Boron"
    elements["C"] = "Carbon"
    elements["N"] = "Nitrogen"
    elements["O"] = "Oxygen"
    elements["F"] = "Fluorine"
    elements["Ne"] = "Neon"

    fmt.Println(elements["Li"])
}
```

`elements` is a map that represents the first 10 chemical elements indexed by their symbol. This is a very common way of using maps: as a lookup table or a dictionary. Suppose we tried to look up an element that doesn't exist:

```go
fmt.Println(elements["Un"])
```

If you run this, you should see nothing returned. Technically, a map returns the zero value for the value type (which for strings is the empty string). Although we could check for the zero value in a condition (`elements["Un"] == ""`), Go provides a better way:

```go
name, ok := elements["Un"]
fmt.Println(name, ok)
```

Accessing an element of a map can return two values instead of just one. The first value is the result of the lookup, the second tells us whether or not the lookup was successful. In Go, we often see code like this:

```
if name, ok := elements["Un"]; ok {
    fmt.Println(name, ok)
}
```

First, we try to get the value from the map. Then, if it's successful, we run the code inside of the block.

Like we saw with arrays, there is also a shorter way to create maps:

```
elements := map[string]string{
    "H":  "Hydrogen",
    "He": "Helium",
    "Li": "Lithium",
    "Be": "Beryllium",
    "B":  "Boron",
    "C":  "Carbon",
    "N":  "Nitrogen",
    "O":  "Oxygen",
    "F":  "Fluorine",
    "Ne": "Neon",
}
```

Maps are also often used to store general information. Let's modify our program so that instead of just storing the name of the element, we store its standard state (state at room temperature) as well:

```
func main() {
    elements := map[string]map[string]string{
        "H": map[string]string{
            "name":"Hydrogen",
            "state":"gas",
        },
        "He": map[string]string{
            "name":"Helium",
            "state":"gas",
        },
        "Li": map[string]string{
            "name":"Lithium",
            "state":"solid",
        },
        "Be": map[string]string{
            "name":"Beryllium",
            "state":"solid",
        },
        "B":  map[string]string{
            "name":"Boron",
            "state":"solid",
        },
        "C":  map[string]string{
            "name":"Carbon",
            "state":"solid",
        },
        "N":  map[string]string{
```

```
                "name":"Nitrogen",
                "state":"gas",
            },
            "O": map[string]string{
                "name":"Oxygen",
                "state":"gas",
            },
            "F": map[string]string{
                "name":"Fluorine",
                "state":"gas",
            },
            "Ne": map[string]string{
                "name":"Neon",
                "state":"gas",
            },
        }

        if el, ok := elements["Li"]; ok {
            fmt.Println(el["name"], el["state"])
        }
    }
```

Notice that the type of our map has changed from `map[string]string` to `map[string]map[string]string`. We now have a map of strings to maps of strings to strings. The outer map is used as a lookup table based on the element's symbol, while the inner maps are used to store general information about the elements. Although maps are often used like this, in Chapter 7 we will see a better way to store structured information.

Exercises

1. How do you access the fourth element of an array or slice?

2. What is the length of a slice created using `make([]int, 3, 9)`?

3. Given the following array, what would `x[2:5]` give you?

   ```
   x := [6]string{"a","b","c","d","e","f"}
   ```

4. Write a program that finds the smallest number in this list:

   ```
   x := []int{
       48,96,86,68,
       57,82,63,70,
       37,34,83,27,
       19,97, 9,17,
   }
   ```

4. Use for loop p 35
                or   p 27

CHAPTER 6

Functions

A function (also known as a procedure or a subroutine) is an independent section of code that maps zero or more input parameters to zero or more output parameters. As illustrated in Figure 6-1, functions are often represented as a black box.

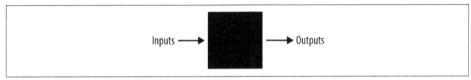

Inputs ⟶ ⟶ Outputs

Figure 6-1. A black box function

In previous chapters, the programs we have written in Go have used only one function:

```
func main() {}
```

We will now begin writing programs that use more than one function.

Your Second Function

Let's take another look at the following program from Chapter 5:

```
func main() {
    xs := []float64{98,93,77,82,83}

    total := 0.0
    for _, v := range xs {          p35  special for
        total += v
    }
    fmt.Println(total / float64(len(xs)))
}
```

This program computes the average of a series of numbers. Finding the average like this is a very general problem, so it's an ideal candidate for definition as a function.

The `average` function will need to take in a slice of `float64`s and return one `float64`. Insert this before the `main` function:

```
func average(xs []float64) float64 {
    panic("Not Implemented")
}
```

Functions start with the keyword `func`, followed by the function's name. The parameters (inputs) of the function are defined like this: `name type, name type, ....` Our function has one parameter (the list of scores) that we named `xs`. After the parameters, we put the return type. Collectively, the parameters and the return type are known as the function's signature.

Finally, we have the function body, which is a series of statements between curly braces. In this body, we invoke a built-in function called `panic` that causes a runtime error (we'll see more about `panic` later in this chapter). Writing functions can be difficult, so it's a good idea to break the process into manageable chunks, rather than trying to implement the entire thing in one large step.

Now let's take the code from our main function and move it into our average function:

```
func average(xs []float64) float64 {
    total := 0.0
    for _, v := range xs {
        total += v
    }
    return total / float64(len(xs))
}
```

Notice that we changed the `fmt.Println` to be a `return` instead. The return statement causes the function to immediately stop and return the value after it to the function that called this one. Modify `main` to look like this:

```
func main() {
    xs := []float64{98,93,77,82,83}
    fmt.Println(average(xs))
}
```

Running this program should give you exactly the same result as the original. A few things to keep in mind:

Parameter names can be different

The calling and callee functions are allowed to use different names for the parameters. For example, we could have done this:

```go
func main() {
    someOtherName := []float64{98,93,77,82,83}
    fmt.Println(average(someOtherName))
}
```

And our program would still work.

Variables must be passed to functions

Functions don't have access to anything in the calling function unless it's passed in explicitly. This won't work:

```go
func f() {
    fmt.Println(x)
}

func main() {
    x := 5
    f()
}
```

We need to either do this:

```go
func f(x int) {
    fmt.Println(x)
}

func main() {
    x := 5
    f(x)
}
```

Or this:

```go
var x int = 5
func f() {
    fmt.Println(x)
}

func main() {
    f()
}
```

Functions form call stacks

Functions are built up in a call *stack*. Suppose we had this program:

```go
func main() {
    fmt.Println(f1())
}

func f1() int {
    return f2()
}
```

```
func f2() int {
    return 1
}
```

We could visualize it as shown in Figure 6-2.

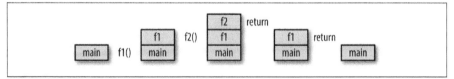

Figure 6-2. A call stack

Each time we call a function, we push it onto the call stack, and each time we return from a function, we pop the last function off of the stack.

Return types can have names

We can name the return type like this:

```
func f2() (r int) {
    r = 1
    return
}
```

Multiple values can be returned

Go is also capable of returning multiple values from a function. Here is an example function that returns two integers:

```
func f() (int, int) {
    return 5, 6
}

func main() {
    x, y := f()
}
```

Three changes are necessary: change the return type to contain multiple types separated by a comma, change the expression after the return so that it contains multiple comma-separated expressions, and finally, change the assignment statement so that multiple values are on the left side of the := or =.

Multiple values are often used to return an error value along with the result (x, err := f()), or a boolean to indicate success (x, ok := f()).

Variadic Functions

There is a special form available for the last parameter in a Go function:

```
func add(args ...int) int {        // Take 0 or more ints
    total := 0
    for _, v := range args {
        total += v
    }
    return total
}

func main() {
    fmt.Println(add(1,2,3))
}
```

In this example, add is allowed to be called with multiple integers. This is known as a *variadic parameter*.

By using an ellipsis (. . .) before the type name of the last parameter, you can indicate that it takes zero or more of those parameters. In this case, we take zero or more ints. We invoke the function like any other function except we can pass as many ints as we want.

This is precisely how the fmt.Println function is implemented:

```
func Println(a ...interface{}) (n int, err error)
```

The Println function takes any number of values of any type (the special interface{} type will be discussed in more detail in Chapter 7).

We can also pass a slice of ints by following the slice with an ellipsis:

```
func main() {
    xs := []int{1,2,3}
    fmt.Println(add(xs...))
}
```

Closure

It is possible to create functions inside of functions. Let's move the add function we saw before inside of main:

```
func main() {
    add := func(x, y int) int {        // add itself is a local variable
        return x + y
    }
    fmt.Println(add(1,1))
}
```

add is a local variable that has the type `func(int, int) int` (a function that takes two ints and returns an int). When you create a local function like this, it also has access to other local variables (remember scope from Chapter 3):

```
func main() {
    x := 0
    increment := func() int {
        x++
        return x
    }
    fmt.Println(increment())
    fmt.Println(increment())
}
```

increment adds 1 to the variable x, which is defined in the main function's scope. This x variable can be accessed and modified by the increment function. This is why the first time we call increment we see 1 displayed, but the second time we call it we see 2 displayed.

A function like this together with the nonlocal variables it references is known as a closure. In this case, increment and the variable x form the closure.

One way to use closure is by writing a function that returns another function, which when called, can generate a sequence of numbers. For example, here's how we might generate all the even numbers:

```
func makeEvenGenerator() func() uint {
    i := uint(0)
    return func() (ret uint) {
        ret = i
        i += 2
        return
    }
}
func main() {
    nextEven := makeEvenGenerator()
    fmt.Println(nextEven()) // 0
    fmt.Println(nextEven()) // 2
    fmt.Println(nextEven()) // 4
}
```

makeEvenGenerator returns a function that generates even numbers. Each time it's called, it adds 2 to the local i variable, which—unlike normal local variables—persists between calls.

Recursion

Finally, a function is able to call itself. Here is one way to compute the factorial of a number:

```
func factorial(x uint) uint {
    if x == 0 {
        return 1
    }
    return x * factorial(x-1)
}
```

`factorial` calls itself, which is what makes this function recursive. In order to better understand how this function works, let's walk through `factorial(2)`:

1. Is x == 0? No (x is 2).
2. Find the factorial of x - 1
   a. Is x == 0? No (x is 1).
   b. Find the `factorial` of x - 1.
      i. Is x == 0? Yes, return 1.
   c. Return 1 * 1.
3. Return 2 * 1.

Closure and recursion are powerful programming techniques that form the basis of a paradigm known as *functional programming*. Most people will find functional programming more difficult to understand than an approach based on for loops, if statements, variables, and simple functions.

defer, panic, and recover

Go has a special statement called defer that schedules a function call to be run after the function completes. Consider the following example:

```
package main

import "fmt"

func first() {
    fmt.Println("1st")
}

func second() {
    fmt.Println("2nd")
}

func main() {
    defer second()
    first()
}
```

This program prints 1st followed by 2nd. Basically, defer moves the call to second to the end of the function:

```
func main() {
    first()
    second()
}
```

defer is often used when resources need to be freed in some way. For example, when we open a file, we need to make sure to close it later. With defer:

```
f, _ := os.Open(filename)
defer f.Close()
```

This has three advantages:

- It keeps our Close call near our Open call so it's easier to understand.
- If our function had multiple return statements (perhaps one in an if and one in an else), Close will happen before both of them.
- Deferred functions are run even if a runtime panic occurs.

panic and recover

Earlier, we created a function that called the panic function to cause a runtime error. We can handle a runtime panic with the built-in recover function. recover stops the panic and returns the value that was passed to the call to panic. We might be tempted to recover from a panic like this:

```
package main

import "fmt"

func main() {
    panic("PANIC")
    str := recover() // this will never happen
    fmt.Println(str)
}
```

But the call to recover will never happen in this case, because the call to panic immediately stops execution of the function. Instead, we have to pair it with defer:

```
package main

import "fmt"

func main() {
    defer func() {
        str := recover()
        fmt.Println(str)
    }()
    panic("PANIC")
}
```

A panic generally indicates a programmer error (e.g., attempting to access an index of an array that's out of bounds, forgetting to initialize a map, etc.) or an exceptional condition that there's no easy way to recover from (hence the name *panic*).

Pointers

When we call a function that takes an argument, that argument is copied to the function:

```go
func zero(x int) {          @
    x = 0
}

func main() {
    x := 5
    zero(x)
    fmt.Println(x) // x is still 5
}
```

In this program, the zero function will not modify the original x variable in the main function. But what if we wanted to? One way to do this is to use a special data type known as a *pointer*:

```go
func zero(xPtr *int) {      @    // Take ptr - to - int
    *xPtr = 0
}
func main() {
    x := 5
    zero(&x)                      // addr of (ptr to) x
    fmt.Println(x) // x is 0
}
```

Pointers reference a location in memory where a value is stored rather than the value itself. By using a pointer (*int), the zero function is able to modify the original variable.

The * and & operators

In Go, a pointer is represented using an asterisk (*) followed by the type of the stored value. In the zero function, xPtr is a pointer to an int.

An asterisk is also used to *dereference* pointer variables. Dereferencing a pointer gives us access to the value the pointer points to. When we write *xPtr = 0, we are saying "store the int 0 in the memory location xPtr refers to." If we try xPtr = 0 instead, we will get a compile-time error because xPtr is not an int; it's a *int, which can only be given another *int.

Finally, we use the & operator to find the address of a variable. &x returns a *int (pointer to an int) because x is an int. This is what allows us to modify the original variable. &x in main and xPtr in zero refer to the same memory location.

new

Another way to get a pointer is to use the built-in new function:

```
func one(xPtr *int) {
    *xPtr = 1
}

func main() {
    xPtr := new(int)
    one(xPtr)
    fmt.Println(*xPtr) // x is 1
}
```

new takes a type as an argument, allocates enough memory to fit a value of that type, and returns a pointer to it.

In some programming languages, there is a significant difference between using new and &, with great care being needed to eventually delete anything created with new. You don't have to worry about this with Go—it's a garbage-collected programming language, which means memory is cleaned up automatically when nothing refers to it anymore.

Pointers are rarely used with Go's built-in types, but as we will see in the next chapter, they are extremely useful when paired with structs.

Exercises   *103*

1. `sum` is a function that takes a slice of numbers and adds them together. What would its function signature look like in Go?   *func sum (xs []int) int*

2. Write a function that takes an integer and halves it and returns true if it was even or false if it was odd. For example, `half(1)` should return (`0`, `false`) and `half(2)` should return (`1`, `true`).

3. Write a function with one variadic parameter that finds the greatest number in a list of numbers.   *func maxInt (args ...int) int*

4. Using `makeEvenGenerator` as an example, write a `makeOddGenerator` function that generates odd numbers.   *p 48*

5. The Fibonacci sequence is defined as: `fib(0)` = `0`, `fib(1)` = `1`, `fib(n)` = `fib(n-1)` + `fib(n-2)`. Write a recursive function that can find `fib(n)`.

6. What are `defer`, `panic`, and `recover`? How do you recover from a runtime panic?

7. How do you get the memory address of a variable?

8. How do you assign a value to a pointer?

9. How do you create a new pointer?

10. What is the value of x after running this program:

```
func square(x *float64) {
    *x = *x * *x
}
func main() {
    x := 1.5
    square(&x)
}
```

11. Write a program that can swap two integers (`x := 1; y := 2; swap(&x, &y)` should give you x=2 and y=1).

CHAPTER 7

Structs and Interfaces

Although it would be possible for us to write programs only using Go's built-in data types, at some point it would become quite tedious. Consider a program that interacts with shapes:

```
package main

import ("fmt"; "math")

func distance(x1, y1, x2, y2 float64) float64 {
    a := x2 - x1
    b := y2 - y1
    return math.Sqrt(a*a + b*b)
}

func rectangleArea(x1, y1, x2, y2 float64) float64 {
    l := distance(x1, y1, x1, y2)
    w := distance(x1, y1, x2, y1)
    return l * w
}

func circleArea(x, y, r float64) float64 {
    return math.Pi * r*r
}

func main() {
    var rx1, ry1 float64 = 0, 0
    var rx2, ry2 float64 = 10, 10
    var cx, cy, cr float64 = 0, 0, 5

    fmt.Println(rectangleArea(rx1, ry1, rx2, ry2))
    fmt.Println(circleArea(cx, cy, cr))
}
```

This program finds the area of a rectangle and a circle. Keeping track of all the coordinates makes it difficult to see what the program is doing and will likely lead to mistakes.

Structs

An easy way to make this program better is to use a struct. A struct is a type that contains named fields. For example, we could represent a circle like this:

```
type Circle struct {
    x float64        // Fields
    y float64
    r float64
}
```

The `type` keyword introduces a new type. It's followed by the name of the type (`Circle`), the keyword `struct` to indicate that we are defining a `struct` type, and a list of fields inside of curly braces.

Fields are like a set of grouped variables. Each field has a name and a type and is stored adjacent to the other fields in the struct. Like with functions, we can collapse fields that have the same type:

```
type Circle struct {
    x, y, r float64
}
```

Initialization

We can create an instance of our new `Circle` type in a variety of ways:

```
var c Circle
```

Like with other data types, this will create a local `Circle` variable that is by default set to zero. For a `struct`, zero means each of the fields is set to their corresponding zero value (0 for `ints`, 0.0 for `floats`, "" for `strings`, `nil` for pointers, etc.) We can also use the `new` function:

```
c := new(Circle)        // pc is a ptr to a Circle st
```

This allocates memory for all the fields, sets each of them to their zero value, and returns a pointer to the struct (`*Circle`). Pointers are often used with structs so that functions can modify their contents.

Using `new` in this way is somewhat uncommon. More typically, we want to give each of the fields an initial value. We can do this in two ways.

The first option looks like this:

```
c := Circle{x: 0, y: 0, r: 5}
```

The second option is to leave off the field names if we know the order they were defined:

```
c := Circle{0, 0, 5}
```

This creates the same `Circle` as the previous example. If you want a pointer to the struct, use &:

```
c := &Circle{0, 0, 5}
```

Fields

We can access fields using the . operator:

```
fmt.Println(c.x, c.y, c.r)
c.x = 10
c.y = 5
```

Let's modify the `circleArea` function so that it uses a `Circle`:

```
func circleArea(c Circle) float64 {
    return math.Pi * c.r*c.r
}
```

In `main`, we have:

```
c := Circle{0, 0, 5}
fmt.Println(circleArea(c))
```

One thing to remember is that arguments are always copied in Go. If we attempted to modify one of the fields inside of the `circleArea` function, it would not modify the original variable. Because of this, we would typically write the function using a pointer to the `Circle`:

```
func circleArea(c *Circle) float64 {
    return math.Pi * c.r*c.r
}
```

And change `main` to use & before c:

```
c := Circle{0, 0, 5}
fmt.Println(circleArea(&c))
```

Methods

Although this is better than the first version of this code, we can improve it significantly by using a special type of function known as a *method*:

```
func (c *Circle) area() float64 {
    return math.Pi * c.r*c.r
}
```

In between the keyword `func` and the name of the function, we've added a *receiver*. The receiver is like a parameter—it has a name and a type—but by creating the function in this way, it allows us to call the function using the . operator:

```
fmt.Println(c.area())
```

This is much easier to read. We no longer need the & operator (Go automatically knows to pass a pointer to the circle for this method), and because this function can only be used with `Circles`, we can rename the function to just `area`.

Let's do the same thing for the rectangle:

```
type Rectangle struct {
    x1, y1, x2, y2 float64
}

func (r *Rectangle) area() float64 {
    l := distance(r.x1, r.y1, r.x1, r.y2)
    w := distance(r.x1, r.y1, r.x2, r.y1)
    return l * w
}
```

`main` has:

```
r := Rectangle{0, 0, 10, 10}
fmt.Println(r.area())
```

Embedded Types

A struct's fields usually represent the has-a relationship (e.g., a `Circle` has a `radius`). The following snippet shows an example of a person struct:

```
type Person struct {
    Name string
}

func (p *Person) Talk() {
    fmt.Println("Hi, my name is", p.Name)
}
```

Now suppose we wanted to create a new `Android` struct. We could do this:

```
type Android struct {
    Person Person
    Model string
}
```

This would work, but we would rather say an android *is* a person, rather than an android *has* a person. Go supports relationships like this by using embedded types (sometimes also referred to as anonymous fields)—they look like this:

```
type Android struct {
    Person                    // embedded type
    Model string
}
```

We use the type (Person) and don't give it a name. When defined this way, the Person struct can be accessed using the type name:

```
a := new(Android)
a.Person.Talk()
```

But we can also call any Person methods directly on the Android:

```
a := new(Android)
a.Talk()
```

The is-a relationship works this way intuitively: people can talk, an android is a person, therefore an android can talk.

Interfaces

You may have noticed that we were able to name the Rectangle's area method the same thing as the Circle's area method. This was no accident. In both real life and in programming, relationships like these are commonplace. Go has a way of making these accidental similarities explicit through a type known as an interface. Here is an example of a Shape interface:

```
type Shape interface {
    area() float64         // method set
}
```

Like a struct, an interface is created using the type keyword, followed by a name and the keyword interface. But instead of defining fields, we define a *method set*. A method set is a list of methods that a type must have in order to *implement* the interface.

In our case, both Rectangle and Circle have area methods that return float64s, so both types implement the Shape interface. By itself, this wouldn't be particularly useful, but we can use interface types as arguments to functions.

Suppose we want to write a function that calculates the area of several shapes. Using the techniques we've discussed so far, we might start to write the function like this:

```
func totalArea(circles ...Circle) float64 {
    var total float64
    for _, c := range circles {
        total += c.area()
    }
    return total
}
```

And then we'd try to add in `Rectangles`:

```
// THIS IS INVALID
func totalArea(circles ...Circle, rectangles ...Rectangle) float64 {
    var total float64
    for _, c := range circles {
        total += c.area()
    }
    for _, r := range rectangles {
        total += r.area()
    }
    return total
}
```

But we can't write a function that contains two variadic parameters, so we would have to modify the program:

```
func totalArea(circles []Circle, rectangles []Rectangle) float64 {
    var total float64
    for _, c := range circles {
        total += c.area()
    }
    for _, r := range rectangles {
        total += r.area()
    }
    return total
}
```

This works, but it has a major issue—whenever we define a new shape, we have to change our function to handle it (a third parameter for `Polygons`, a fourth for `Squares`, etc.).

This is the problem interfaces are designed to solve. Because both of our shapes have an `area` method, they both implement the `Shape` interface and we can change our function to this:

```
func totalArea(shapes ...Shape) float64 {
    var area float64
    for _, s := range shapes {
        area += s.area()
    }
    return area
}
```

We would call this function like this:

```
fmt.Println(totalArea(&c, &r))
```

All `totalArea` knows about each shape is that it has an `area` method:

```
type Shape interface {
    area() float64
}
```

So `totalArea` would not be able to access the struct fields for the circle or rectangle (or any other possible methods).

Nothing additional is required to implement an interface (there is no `implements` or `extends` keyword). It's sufficient to merely have a method with the same name and signature.

Interfaces can also be used as fields. Consider a `MultiShape` that is made up of several smaller shapes:

```
type MultiShape struct {
    shapes []Shape
}
```

We can create a `MultiShape` like this:

```
multiShape := MultiShape{
    shapes: []Shape{
        Circle{0, 0, 5},
        Rectangle{0, 0, 10, 10},
    },
}
```

We can even turn `MultiShape` itself into a `Shape` by giving it an area method:

```
func (m *MultiShape) area() float64 {
    var area float64
    for _, s := range m.shapes {
        area += s.area()
    }
    return area
}
```

Now a `MultiShape` can contain `Circles`, `Rectangles`, or even other `MultiShapes`.

When building new programs, you often won't know what your types should look like when you start—and that's OK. In Go, you generally focus more on the behavior of your program than on a taxonomy of types. Create a few small structs that do what you want, add in methods that you need, and as you build your program, useful interfaces will tend to emerge. There's no need to have them all figured out ahead of time.

Interfaces are particularly useful as software projects grow and become more complex. They allow us to hide the incidental details of implementation (e.g., the fields of our struct), which makes it easier to reason about software components in isolation. In our example, as long as the `area` methods we defined continue to produce the same results, we're free to change how a `Circle` or `Rectangle` is structured without having to worry about whether or not the `totalArea` function will continue to work.

Go also has a mechanism for combining interfaces, types, variables, and functions together into a single component known as a *package*. We will learn more about packages in the next chapter.

Exercises

1. What's the difference between a method and a function?

2. Why would you use an embedded anonymous field instead of a normal named field?

3. Add a new `perimeter` method to the `Shape` interface to calculate the perimeter of a shape. Implement the method for `Circle` and `Rectangle`.

CHAPTER 8

Packages

Go was designed to be a language that encourages good software engineering practices. An important part of high-quality software is code reuse—embodied in the principle "Don't Repeat Yourself."

As we saw in Chapter 6, functions are the first layer we utilize to allow code reuse. Go also provides another mechanism for code reuse: packages. Nearly every program we've seen so far included this line:

```
import "fmt"
```

fmt is the name of a package that includes a variety of functions related to formatting and output to the screen. Bundling code in this way serves three purposes:

- It reduces the chance of having overlapping names, and in turn keeps our function names short and succinct.   *// "namespacing*
- It organizes code so that it's easier to find code you want to reuse.   *// organize*
- It speeds up the compiler by only requiring recompilation of smaller chunks of a program. Although we use the package fmt, we don't have to recompile it every time we change our program.   *// pre-compilation*

The Core Packages

Instead of writing everything from scratch, most real-world programming depends on our ability to interface with existing libraries. This chapter will take a look at some of the most commonly used packages included with Go.

First, a word of warning: although some of these libraries are fairly obvious (or have been explained in previous chapters), many of the libraries included with Go require

63

specialized, domain-specific knowledge (e.g., cryptography). It is beyond the scope of this book to explain these underlying technologies.

Strings

Go includes a large number of functions to work with strings in the `strings` package.

To search for a smaller string in a bigger string, use the `Contains` function:

Contains

```
package main

import (
    "fmt"
    "strings"
)

func main() {
    // Contains(s, substr string) bool
    fmt.Println(strings.Contains("test", "es"))
    // => true
}
```

To count the number of times a smaller string occurs in a bigger string, use the `Count` function:

Count

```
package main

import (
    "fmt"
    "strings"
)

func main() {
    // func Count(s, sep string) int
    fmt.Println(strings.Count("test", "t"))
    // => 2
}
```

To determine if a bigger string starts with a smaller string, use the `HasPrefix` function:

Has Prefix

```
package main

import (
    "fmt"
    "strings"
)

func main() {
    // func HasPrefix(s, prefix string) bool
    fmt.Println(strings.HasPrefix("test", "te"))
```

```
    // => true
}
```

To determine if a bigger string ends with a smaller string, use the HasSuffix function:

```
package main

import (
    "fmt"
    "strings"
)

func main() {
    // func HasSuffix(s, suffix string) bool
    fmt.Println(strings.HasSuffix("test", "st"))
    // => true
}
```

Has Suffix

To find the position of a smaller string in a bigger string, use the Index function (it returns -1 if not found):

```
package main

import (
    "fmt"
    "strings"
)

func main() {
    // func Index(s, sep string) int
    fmt.Println(strings.Index("test", "e"))
    // => 1
}
```

To take a list of strings and join them together in a single string separated by another string (e.g., a comma), use the Join function:

```
package main

import (
    "fmt"
    "strings"
)

func main() {
    // func Join(a []string, sep string) string
    fmt.Println(strings.Join([]string{"a","b"}, "-"))
    // => "a-b"
}
```

Join

To repeat a string, use the Repeat function:

```
package main

import (
    "fmt"
    "strings"
)
```

Repeat

```
func main() {
    // func Repeat(s string, count int) string
    fmt.Println(strings.Repeat("a", 5))
    // => "aaaaa"
}
```

To replace a smaller string in a bigger string with some other string, use the `Replace` function. In Go, `Replace` also takes a number indicating how many times to do the replacement (pass -1 to do it as many times as possible):

```
package main

import (
    "fmt"
    "strings"
)
```

Replace

```
func main() {
    // func Replace(s, old, new string, n int) string
    fmt.Println(strings.Replace("aaaa", "a", "b", 2))
    // => "bbaa"
}
```

To split a string into a list of strings by a separating string (e.g., a comma), use the `Split` function (`Split` is the reverse of `Join`):

```
package main

import (
    "fmt"
    "strings"
)
```

Split

```
func main() {
    // func Split(s, sep string) []string
    fmt.Println(strings.Split("a-b-c-d-e", "-")))
    // => []string{"a","b","c","d","e"}
}
```

To convert a string to all lowercase letters, use the `ToLower` function:

```
package main

import (
    "fmt"
    "strings"
```

ToLower

```
)

func main() {
    // func ToLower(s string) string
    // fmt.Println(strings.ToLower("TEST"))
    // => "test"
}
```

To convert a string to all uppercase letters, use the ToUpper function:

```
package main

import (
    "fmt"
    "strings"
)

func main() {
    // func ToUpper(s string) string
    // fmt.Println(strings.ToUpper("test"))
    // => "TEST"
}
```

To Upper

Sometimes we need to work with strings as binary data. To convert a string to a slice of bytes (and vice versa), do this:

```
arr := []byte("test")
str := string([]byte{'t','e','s','t'})
```

Input/Output   *io package*

Before we look at files, we need to understand Go's io package. The io package consists of a few functions, but mostly interfaces used in other packages. The two main interfaces are Reader and Writer. Readers support reading via the Read method. Writers support writing via the Write method. Many functions in Go take Readers or Writers as arguments. For example, the io package has a Copy function that copies data from a Reader to a Writer:

```
func Copy(dst Writer, src Reader) (written int64, err error)
```

from

To read or write to a []byte or a string, you can use the Buffer struct found in the bytes package: *bytes package*

```
var buf bytes.Buffer
buf.Write([]byte("test"))    // write byte array "constructed from string 'test'" to buf
```

A Buffer doesn't have to be initialized, and it supports both the Reader and Writer interfaces. You can convert it into a []byte by calling buf.Bytes(). If you only need to read from a string, you can also use the strings.NewReader function, which is more efficient than using a buffer.

Files and Folders

To open a file in Go, use the Open function from the os package. Here is an example
of how to read the contents of a file and display them on the terminal:

```go
package main        "os" package

import (
    "fmt"
    "os"
)

func main() {
    file, err := os.Open("test.txt")
    if err != nil {
        // handle the error here
        return
    }
    defer file.Close()

    // get the file size
    stat, err := file.Stat()      // get stat struct for file
    if err != nil {
        return
    }
    // read the file
    bs := make([]byte, stat.Size())   // init a bytes buffer of size == file's size
    _, err = file.Read(bs)            // read file bytes into bytes buffer
    if err != nil {
        return
    }

    str := string(bs)    // convert bytes buffer to string
    fmt.Println(str)
}
```

We use defer file.Close() right after opening the file to make sure the file is closed
as soon as the function completes. Reading files is very common, so there's a shorter
way to do this:

```go
package main        "io/ioutil" package

import (
    "fmt"
    "io/ioutil"
)

func main() {
    bs, err := ioutil.ReadFile("test.txt")
    if err != nil {
        return
    }
```

```
    str := string(bs)
    fmt.Println(str)
}
```

To create a file, use the os.Create function. It takes the name of the file, creates it in the current working directory, and returns an os.File and possibly an error (if it was unable to create it for some reason). Here's an example program:

```
package main

import (
    "os"
)

func main() {
    file, err := os.Create("test.txt")
    if err != nil {
        // handle the error here
        return
    }
    defer file.Close()

    file.WriteString("test")      // Write string "test" to new file
}
```

To get the contents of a directory, we use the same os.Open function but give it a directory path instead of a file name. Then we call the Readdir method:

```
package main

import (
    "fmt"
    "os"
)

func main() {
    dir, err := os.Open(".")
    if err != nil {
        return
    }
    defer dir.Close()

    fileInfos, err := dir.Readdir(-1)      // -1 => return all dir entries
    if err != nil {
        return
    }
    for _, fi := range fileInfos {
        fmt.Println(fi.Name())
    }
}
```

Readdir takes a single argument that limits the number of entries returned. By passing in -1, we return all of the entries.

Often, we want to recursively walk a folder (read the folder's contents, all the subfolders, all the sub-subfolders, etc.). To make this easier, there's a Walk function provided in the path/filepath package:

```
package main                  "path/filepath" package

import (
    "fmt"
    "os"
    "path/filepath"
)

func main() {
    filepath.Walk(".", func(path string, info os.FileInfo, err error) error {
        fmt.Println(path)
        return nil
    })
}
```

The function you pass to Walk is called for every file and folder in the root folder (in this case, .). It's passed three arguments: path, which is the path to the file; info, which is the information for the file (the same information you get from using os.Stat); and err, which is any error that was received while walking the directory. (If) The function returns an error and you can return filepath.SkipDir to stop walking immediately.

Errors

Go has a built-in type for errors that we have already seen (the error type). We can create our own errors by using the New function in the errors package:

```
package main                  "errors" package

import "errors"

func main() {
    err := errors.New("error message")
}
```

Containers and Sort

In addition to lists and maps, Go has several more collections available underneath the container package. We'll take a look at the container/list package as an example.

List

The container/list package implements a doubly linked list. A linked list is a type
of data structure that looks like Figure 8-1.

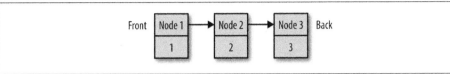

Figure 8-1. A linked list

Each node of the list contains a value (1, 2, or 3, in this case) and a pointer to the next
node. Because this is a doubly linked list, each node will also have pointers to the previous node. This list could be created by this program:

```
package main              is "containers/list"   package

import ("fmt" ; "container/list")

func main() {
    var x list.List       // create empty list
    x.PushBack(1)
    x.PushBack(2)
    x.PushBack(3)

    for e := x.Front(); e != nil; e=e.Next() {
        fmt.Println(e.Value.(int))
    }
}
```

The zero value for a List is an empty list (a *List can also be created using
list.New). Values are appended to the list using PushBack. We loop over each item in
the list by getting the first element, and following all the links until we reach nil.

Sort

The sort package contains functions for sorting arbitrary data. There are several predefined sorting functions (for slices of ints and floats) Here's an example for how to
sort your own data:

```
package main

import ("fmt" ; "sort")

type Person struct {
    Name string
    Age int
}

type ByName []Person
```

```
                 receiver
func (ps ByName) Len() int {
    return len(ps)
}
func (ps ByName) Less(i, j int) bool {
    return ps[i].Name < ps[j].Name
}
func (ps ByName) Swap(i, j int) {
    ps[i], ps[j] = ps[j], ps[i]
}

func main() {
    kids := []Person{
        {"Jill",9},
        {"Jack",10},
    }
    sort.Sort(ByName(kids))      // Cast kids ([]Person) to ByName
    fmt.Println(kids)
}
```

The Sort function in sort takes a sort.Interface and sorts it. The sort.Interface requires three methods: Len, Less, and Swap.

Len should return the length of the thing we are sorting. For a slice, simply return len(ps).

Less is used to determine whether the item at position i is strictly less than the item at position j. In this case, we simply compare ps[i].Name to ps[j].Name.

Swap swaps the items.

To define our own sort, we create a new type (ByName) and make it equivalent to a slice of what we want to sort. We then define the three methods.

Sorting our list of people is then as easy as casting the list into our new type. We could also sort by age by doing this:

```
type ByAge []Person
func (this ByAge) Len() int {
    return len(this)
}
func (this ByAge) Less(i, j int) bool {
    return this[i].Age < this[j].Age
}
func (this ByAge) Swap(i, j int) {
    this[i], this[j] = this[j], this[i]
}
```

Hashes and Cryptography

A hash function takes a set of data and reduces it to a smaller fixed size. Hashes are frequently used in programming for everything from looking up data to easily detecting changes. Hash functions in Go are broken into two categories: cryptographic and non-cryptographic.

The non-cryptographic hash functions can be found underneath the hash package and include adler32, crc32, crc64, and fnv. Here's an example using crc32:

```
package main                    "hash/crc32" package

import (
    "fmt"
    "hash/crc32"
)

func main() {
    // create a hasher
    h := crc32.NewIEEE()        ←
    // write our data to it
    h.Write([]byte("test"))
    // calculate the crc32 checksum
    v := h.Sum32()
    fmt.Println(v)
}
```

The crc32 hash object implements the Writer interface, so we can write bytes to it like any other Writer. Once we've written everything we want, we call Sum32() to return a uint32. A common use for crc32 is to compare two files. If the Sum32 value for both files is the same, it's highly likely (though not 100% certain) that the files are the same. If the values are different, then the files are definitely not the same:

```
package main

import (
    "fmt"
    "hash/crc32"
    "io/ioutil"
)

func getHash(filename string) (uint32, error) {
    // open the file
    f, err := os.Open(filename)
    if err != nil {
        return 0, err
    }
    // remember to always close opened files
    defer f.Close()

    // create a hasher
```

```
    h := crc32.NewIEEE()
    // copy the file into the hasher
    // - copy takes (dst, src) and returns (bytesWritten, error)
    _, err := io.Copy(h, f)
    // we don't care about how many bytes were written, but we do want to
    // handle the error
    if err != nil {
      return 0, err
    }
    return h.Sum32(), nil
}

func main() {
    h1, err := getHash("test1.txt")
    if err != nil {
        return
    }
    h2, err := getHash("test2.txt")
    if err != nil {
        return
    }
    fmt.Println(h1, h2, h1 == h2)
}
```

Cryptographic hash functions are similar to their non-cryptographic counterparts, but they have the added property of being hard to reverse. Given the cryptographic hash of a set of data, it's extremely difficult to determine what made the hash. These hashes are often used in security applications.

One common cryptographic hash function is known as SHA-1. Here's how it is used:

```
package main

import (                   " crypto / sha1 "  package
    "fmt"
    "crypto/sha1"
)

func main() {
    h := sha1.New()
    h.Write([]byte("test"))
    bs := h.Sum([]byte{})
    fmt.Println(bs)
}
```

This example is very similar to the crc32 one, because both crc32 and sha1 implement the hash.Hash interface. The main difference is that whereas crc32 computes a 32-bit hash, sha1 computes a 160-bit hash. There is no native type to represent a 160-bit number, so we use a slice of 20 bytes instead.

Servers

Writing distributed, networked applications in Go is relatively straightforward. We will briefly take a look at three common approaches to communicating between multiple computers: TCP servers, HTTP servers, and RPC.

TCP

TCP is the primary protocol used for communication over the Internet. Any time you interact with a web page, play a multiplayer computer game, stream a movie, or video chat, there's a good chance your computer is communicating with a remote server using TCP.

In Go, we can create a TCP server using the net package's Listen function. Listen takes a network type (in our case, tcp) and an address and port to bind, and returns a net.Listener:

```
type Listener interface {
    // Accept waits for and returns the next connection to the listener.
    Accept() (c Conn, err error)

    // Close closes the listener.
    // Any blocked Accept operations will be unblocked and return errors.
    Close() error

    // Addr returns the listener's network address.
    Addr() Addr
}
```

Once we have a Listener, we call Accept, which waits for a client to connect and returns a net.Conn. A net.Conn implements the io.Reader and io.Writer interfaces, so we can read from it and write to it just like a file.

Here's a complete example:

```
package main

import (
    "encoding/gob"
    "fmt"
    "net"
)

func server() {
    // listen on a port
    ln, err := net.Listen("tcp", ":9999")
    if err != nil {
        fmt.Println(err)
        return
    }
```

```go
    for {
        // accept a connection
        c, err := ln.Accept()
        if err != nil {
          fmt.Println(err)
          continue
        }
        // handle the connection
        go handleServerConnection(c)
    }
}

func handleServerConnection(c net.Conn) {
    // receive the message
    var msg string
    err := gob.NewDecoder(c).Decode(&msg)    // decode into string msg
    if err != nil {
        fmt.Println(err)
    } else {
        fmt.Println("Received", msg)
    }
    c.Close()
}

func client() {                              func client()
    // connect to the server
    c, err := net.Dial("tcp", "127.0.0.1:9999")
    if err != nil {
        fmt.Println(err)
        return
    }

    // send the message
    msg := "Hello, World"
    fmt.Println("Sending", msg)
    err = gob.NewEncoder(c).Encode(msg)
    if err != nil {
        fmt.Println(err)
    }

    c.Close()
}

func main() {
    go server()
    go client()

    var input string
    fmt.Scanln(&input)
}
```

This example uses the encoding/gob package, which makes it easy to encode Go values so that other Go programs (or the same Go program, in this case) can read them. Additional encodings are available in packages underneath encoding (like encoding/json) as well as in third-party packages (e.g., we could use labix.org/v2/mgo/bson for bson support).

HTTP

HTTP servers are even easier to set up and use:

```
package main                              "net/http"  package

import ("net/http" ; "io")

func hello(res http.ResponseWriter, req *http.Request) {
    res.Header().Set(
        "Content-Type",
        "text/html",
    )
    io.WriteString(
        res,
        `<DOCTYPE html>
        <html>
          <head>
              <title>Hello, World</title>
          </head>
          <body>
              Hello, World!
          </body>
        </html>`,
    )
}
func main() {
    http.HandleFunc("/hello", hello)
    http.ListenAndServe(":9000", nil)
}
```

HandleFunc handles a URL route (/hello) by calling the given function. We can also handle static files by using FileServer:

```
http.Handle(
    "/assets/",
    http.StripPrefix(
        "/assets/",
        http.FileServer(http.Dir("assets")),
    ),
)
```

RPC

The net/rpc (remote procedure call) and net/rpc/jsonrpc packages provide an easy way to expose methods so they can be invoked over a network (rather than just in the program running them):

[handwritten: "net/rpc"]
[handwritten: "net/rpc/jsonrpc" package]

```go
package main

import (
    "fmt"
    "net"
    "net/rpc"
)

type Server struct {}
func (this *Server) Negate(i int64, reply *int64) error {
    *reply = -i
    return nil
}

func server() {
    rpc.Register(new(Server))
    ln, err := net.Listen("tcp", ":9999")
    if err != nil {
        fmt.Println(err)
        return
    }
    for {
        c, err := ln.Accept()
        if err != nil {
            continue
        }
        go rpc.ServeConn(c)
    }
}
func client() {
    c, err := rpc.Dial("tcp", "127.0.0.1:9999")
    if err != nil {
        fmt.Println(err)
        return
    }
    var result int64
    err = c.Call("Server.Negate", int64(999), &result)
    if err != nil {
        fmt.Println(err)
    } else {
        fmt.Println("Server.Negate(999) =", result)
    }
}
func main() {
    go server()
    go client()
```

```
    var input string
    fmt.Scanln(&input)
}
```

This program is similar to the TCP example, except now we created an object to hold all the methods we want to expose and we call the Negate method from the client. See the documentation in net/rpc for more details.

Parsing Command-Line Arguments

When we invoke a command on the terminal, it's possible to pass that command arguments. We've seen this with the go command:

```
go run myfile.go
```

run and myfile.go are arguments. We can also pass flags to a command:

```
go run -v myfile.go
```

The flag package allows us to parse arguments and flags sent to our program. Here's an example program that generates a number between 0 and 6. We can change the max value by sending a flag (-max=100) to the program:

```
package main

import ("fmt";"flag";"math/rand")

func main() {
    // Define flags
    maxp := flag.Int("max", 6, "the max value")
    // Parse
    flag.Parse()
    // Generate a number between 0 and max
    fmt.Println(rand.Intn(*maxp))
}
```

Any additional non-flag arguments can be retrieved with flag.Args(), which returns a []string.

Creating Packages

Packages only really make sense in the context of a separate program that uses them. Without this separate program, we have no way of using the package we create. Let's create an application that will use a package we will write. Create a folder in ~/src/ golang-book called chapter8. Inside that folder, create a file called main.go using the following code:

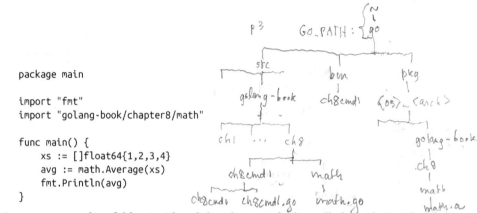

```go
package main

import "fmt"
import "golang-book/chapter8/math"

func main() {
    xs := []float64{1,2,3,4}
    avg := math.Average(xs)
    fmt.Println(avg)
}
```

Now create another folder inside of the *chapter8* folder called *math*. Inside of this folder, create a file called *math.go* that contains this:

```go
package math

func Average(xs []float64) float64 {
    total := float64(0)
    for _, x := range xs {
        total += x
    }
    return total / float64(len(xs))
}
```

Using a terminal, change directory into the *math* folder you just created and run go install. This will compile the math.go program and create a linkable object file: */pkg/os_arch/golang-book/chapter8/math.a* (where *os* is something like *windows* and *arch* is something like *amd64*).

Now change back into the *chapter8* folder and run go run main.go. You should see 2.5. Some things to note:

- math is the name of a package that is part of Go's standard distribution, but because Go packages can be hierarchical, we are safe to use the same name for our package (the real math package is just math, ours is golang-book/chapter8/math).

- When we import our math library, we use its full name (import "golang-book/chapter8/math"), but inside of the *math.go* file, we only use the last part of the name (package math).

- We also only use the short name math when we reference functions from our library. If we wanted to use both libraries in the same program, Go allows us to use an alias (m is the alias):

```go
import m "golang-book/chapter8/math"

func main() {
    xs := []float64{1,2,3,4}
    avg := m.Average(xs)
```

```
    fmt.Println(avg)
}
```

- You may have noticed that every function in the packages we've seen starts with a capital letter. In Go, if something starts with a capital letter, that means other packages (and programs) are able to see it. If we had named the function `average` instead of `Average`, our `main` program would not have been able to see it. ✗

  It's a good practice to only expose the parts of our package that we want other packages using and hide everything else. This allows us to freely change those parts later without having to worry about breaking other programs, and it makes our package easier to use.

- Package names match the folders they fall in. There are ways around this, but it's a lot easier if you stay within this pattern. *Convention*

Documentation

Go has the ability to automatically generate documentation for packages we write in a similar way to the standard package documentation. In a terminal, run this command:

```
godoc golang-book/chapter8/math Average
```

You should see information displayed for the function we just wrote:

```
func Average(xs []float64) float64
```

We can improve this documentation by adding a comment before the function: *@ 80*

```
// Finds the average of a series of numbers
func Average(xs []float64) float64 {
```

If you rerun the `godoc` command, you should see our comment below the function definition:

```
func Average(xs []float64) float64
    Finds the average of a series of numbers
```

This documentation is also available in web form by running this command: ✗

```
godoc -http=":6060"
```

and entering this URL into your browser:

```
http://localhost:6060/pkg/
```

You should be able to browse through all of the packages installed on your system.

Exercises

1. Why do we use packages?

2. What is the difference between an identifier that starts with a capital letter and one that doesn't (e.g., `Average` versus `average`)?

3. What is a package alias? How do you make one?

4. We copied the `average` function from Chapter 6 to our new package. Create `Min` and `Max` functions that find the minimum and maximum values in a slice of `float64s`.

5. How would you document the functions you created in #4?

CHAPTER 9

Testing

Programming is not easy; even the best programmers are incapable of writing programs that work exactly as intended every time. Therefore, an important part of the software development process is testing. Writing tests for our code is a good way to ensure quality and improve reliability.

Go includes a special program that makes writing tests easier: go test. To illustrate how go test works, let's create some tests for the package we made in Chapter 8. In the *chapter8/math* folder, create a new file called *math_test.go*. The Go compiler knows to ignore code in any files that end with *_test.go*, so the code defined in this file is only used by go test (and not go install or go build).

The *~/src/golang-book/chapter8/math/math_test.go* file should contain the same package math we saw before:

```
package math
```

Then we import the special testing package and define a function that starts with the word Test (case matters) followed by whatever we want to name our test. We'll be testing the Average function we wrote before, so let's name it TestAverage:

```
package math

import "testing"

func TestAverage(t *testing.T) {
    v := Average([]float64{1,2})
    if v != 1.5 {
        t.Error("Expected 1.5, got ", v)
    }
}
```

For the body of the function, we invoke the `Average` function on a hardcoded slice of floats (`Average([]float64{1,2})`). We then take that value and compare it to `1.5` and if they're not the same, we use the special `t.Error` function (which is very much like `fmt.Println`) to signal an error to the `go test` program.

To actually run the test, run the following in the same directory:

```
go test
```

You should see this:

```
$ go test
PASS
ok      golang-book/chapter8/math      0.032s
```

The `go test` command will look for any tests in any of the files in the current folder and run them. Tests are identified by starting a function with the word `Test` and taking one argument of type `*testing.T`.

Once we have set up the testing function, we write tests that use the code we're testing. In this case, we know the average of `[1,2]` should be `1.5` so that's what we check. It's probably a good idea to test many different combinations of numbers, so let's slightly modify our test program:

```go
package math

import "testing"

type testpair struct {
    values  []float64
    average float64
}

var tests = []testpair{
    { []float64{1,2}, 1.5 },
    { []float64{1,1,1,1,1,1}, 1 },
    { []float64{-1,1}, 0 },
}

func TestAverage(t *testing.T) {
    for _, pair := range tests {
        v := Average(pair.values)
        if v != pair.average {
            t.Error(
                "For", pair.values,
                "expected", pair.average,
                "got", v,
            )
        }
    }
}
```

This is a very common way to set up tests (abundant examples can be found in the source code for the packages included with Go). We create a `struct` to represent the inputs and outputs for the function:

```
type testpair struct {
    values []float64
    average float64
}
```

Then we create a list of these `testpairs`, loop through each one, and run the function:

```
for _, pair := range tests {
    v := Average(pair.values)
    if v != pair.average {
        t.Error(
            "For", pair.values,
            "expected", pair.average,
            "got", v,
        )
    }
}
```

Creating a good set of tests, and in particular, knowing precisely which values to test, takes a bit of practice. For a list of floating-point numbers, it's a good idea to test a variety of cases: an empty list, several random values, repeated or negative numbers, and so on. But even a small set of basic tests is better than none.

Exercises

1. Writing a good suite of tests is not always easy, but the process of writing tests often reveals more about a problem than you may at first realize. For example, with our Average function, what happens if you pass in an empty list ([]float64{})? How could the function be modified to return 0 in this case?

2. Write a series of tests for the Min and Max functions you wrote in the previous chapter.

CHAPTER 10

Concurrency

Large programs are often made up of many smaller subprograms. For example, a web server handles requests made from web browsers and serves up HTML web pages in response. Each request is handled like a small program.

It would be ideal for programs like these to be able to run their smaller components at the same time (in the case of the web server, to handle multiple requests). Making progress on more than one task simultaneously is known as *concurrency*. Go has rich support for concurrency using goroutines and channels.

Goroutines

A goroutine is a function that is capable of running concurrently with other functions. To create a goroutine, we use the keyword go followed by a function invocation:

```go
package main

import "fmt"

func f(n int) {
    for i := 0; i < 10; i++ {
        fmt.Println(n, ":", i)
    }
}

func main() {
    go f(0)
    var input string
    fmt.Scanln(&input)
}
```

This program consists of two goroutines. The first goroutine is implicit and is the main function itself. The second goroutine is created when we call go f(0). Normally, when we invoke a function, our program will execute all the statements in a function and then return to the next line following the invocation. With a goroutine, we return immediately to the next line and don't wait for the function to complete. This is why the call to the Scanln function has been included; without it, the program would exit before being given the opportunity to print all the numbers.

Goroutines are lightweight and we can easily create thousands of them. We can modify our program to run 10 goroutines by doing this:

```go
func main() {
    for i := 0; i < 10; i++ {
        go f(i)
    }
    var input string
    fmt.Scanln(&input)
}
```

You may have noticed that when you run this program it seems to run the goroutines in order rather than simultaneously. Let's add some delay to the function using time.Sleep and rand.Intn:

```go
package main

import (
    "fmt"
    "time"
    "math/rand"
)

func f(n int) {
    for i := 0; i < 10; i++ {
        fmt.Println(n, ":", i)
        amt := time.Duration(rand.Intn(250))
        time.Sleep(time.Millisecond * amt)
    }
}

func main() {
    for i := 0; i < 10; i++ {
        go f(i)
    }
    var input string
    fmt.Scanln(&input)
}
```

When run, this program produces the following:

```
4 : 0      // err: numbers should be reversed --. 0:4
6 : 0
5 : 0
7 : 0
0 : 0
8 : 0
2 : 0
3 : 0
1 : 0
9 : 0
3 : 1
9 : 1
7 : 1
9 : 2
8 : 1
0 : 1
4 : 1
5 : 1
```

f prints out the numbers from 0 to 10, waiting between 0 and 250 ms after each one. The goroutines should now run simultaneously.

Channels

Channels provide a way for two goroutines to communicate with each other and synchronize their execution. Here is an example program using channels:

```go
package main

import (
    "fmt"
    "time"
)

func pinger(c chan string) {
    for i := 0; ; i++ {
        c <- "ping"
    }
}

func printer(c chan string) {
    for {
        msg := <- c
        fmt.Println(msg)
        time.Sleep(time.Second * 1)
    }
}
```

```
func main() {
    var c chan string = make(chan string)

    go pinger(c)
    go printer(c)

    var input string
    fmt.Scanln(&input)
}
```

This program will print ping forever (hit Enter to stop it). A channel type is represented with the keyword chan followed by the type of the things that are passed on the channel (in this case, we are passing strings). The left arrow operator (<-) is used to send and receive messages on the channel. c <- "ping" means send "ping". msg := <- c means receive a message and store it in msg. The fmt line could also have been written like fmt.Println(<-c), in which case we could remove the previous line.

Using a channel like this synchronizes the two goroutines. When pinger attempts to send a message on the channel, it will wait until printer is ready to receive the message (this is known as *blocking*). Let's add another sender to the program and see what happens. Add this function:

```
func ponger(c chan string) {
    for i := 0; ; i++ {
        c <- "pong"
    }
}
```

And modify main:

```
func main() {
    var c chan string = make(chan string)

    go pinger(c)
    go ponger(c)
    go printer(c)

    var input string    } // delay for user input
    fmt.Scanln(&input)  }
}
```

The program will now take turns printing ping and pong.

Channel Direction

We can specify a direction on a channel type, thus restricting it to either sending or receiving. For example, pinger's function signature can be changed to this:

```
func pinger(c chan<- string)
```

Now pinger is only allowed to send to c. Attempting to receive from c will result in a compile-time error. Similarly, we can change printer to this:

```
func printer(c <-chan string)
```

A channel that doesn't have these restrictions is known as *bidirectional*. A bidirectional channel can be passed to a function that takes send-only or receive-only channels, but the reverse is not true.

Select

Go has a special statement called select that works like a switch but for channels:

```
func main() {
    c1 := make(chan string)
    c2 := make(chan string)

    go func() {
        for {
            c1 <- "from 1"
            time.Sleep(time.Second * 2)
        }
    }()

    go func() {
        for {
            c2 <- "from 2"
            time.Sleep(time.Second * 3)
        }
    }()

    go func() {
        for {
            select {
            case msg1 := <- c1:
                fmt.Println(msg1)
            case msg2 := <- c2:
                fmt.Println(msg2)
            }
        }
    }()

    var input string
```

```
    fmt.Scanln(&input)
}
```

This program prints "from 1" every 2 seconds and "from 2" every 3 seconds. `select` picks the first channel that is ready and receives from it (or sends to it). If more than one of the channels are ready, then it randomly picks which one to receive from. If none of the channels are ready, the statement blocks until one becomes available.

The `select` statement is often used to implement a timeout:

```
select {
case msg1 := <- c1:
    fmt.Println("Message 1", msg1)
case msg2 := <- c2:
    fmt.Println("Message 2", msg2)
case <- time.After(time.Second):
    fmt.Println("timeout")
}
```

`time.After` creates a channel, and after the given duration, will send the current time on it (we weren't interested in the time, so we didn't store it in a variable). We can also specify a `default` case:

```
select {
case msg1 := <- c1:
    fmt.Println("Message 1", msg1)
case msg2 := <- c2:
    fmt.Println("Message 2", msg2)
case <- time.After(time.Second):
    fmt.Println("timeout")
default:
    fmt.Println("nothing ready")
}
```

The default case happens immediately if none of the channels are ready.

Buffered Channels

It's also possible to pass a second parameter to the `make` function when creating a channel:

```
c := make(chan int, 1)
```

This creates a buffered channel with a capacity of 1. Normally, channels are synchronous; both sides of the channel will wait until the other side is ready. A buffered channel is asynchronous; sending or receiving a message will not wait unless the channel is already full. If the channel is full, then sending will wait until there is room for at least one more `int`.

An Example

Here is an example program that uses goroutines and channels. It fetches several web pages simultaneously using the net/http package, and prints the URL of the biggest home page (defined as the most bytes in the response):

```go
package main

import (
    "fmt"
    "io/ioutil"
    "net/http"
)

type HomePageSize struct {
    URL  string
    Size int
}

func main() {
    urls := []string{
        "http://www.apple.com",
        "http://www.amazon.com",
        "http://www.google.com",
        "http://www.microsoft.com",
    }

    results := make(chan HomePageSize)    // results channel

    for _, url := range urls {
        go func(url string) {             // anonymous func ...
            res, err := http.Get(url)
            if err != nil {
                panic(err)
            }
            defer res.Body.Close()

            bs, err := ioutil.ReadAll(res.Body)
            if err != nil {
                panic(err)
            }

            results <- HomePageSize{
                URL:  url,
                Size: len(bs),
            }
        }(url)                            // ... that is invoked immediately
    }

    var biggest HomePageSize

    for range urls {
```

```
        result := <-results
        if result.Size > biggest.Size {
            biggest = result
        }
    }

    fmt.Println("The biggest home page:", biggest.URL)
}
```

We define a type that will store home page sizes:

```
type HomePageSize struct {
    URL  string
    Size int
}
```

Then we create a list of URLs:

```
urls := []string{
    "http://www.apple.com",
    "http://www.amazon.com",
    "http://www.google.com",
    "http://www.microsoft.com",
}
```

Then we create a channel and start a new goroutine for each URL (so we will be fetching four URLs simultaneously). For each URL, we make an HTTP get request:

```
res, err := http.Get(url)
if err != nil {
    panic(err)
}
defer res.Body.Close()
```

And we store the size of the response body:

```
bs, err := ioutil.ReadAll(res.Body)
if err != nil {
    panic(err)
}

results <- HomePageSize{
    URL:  url,
    Size: len(bs),
}
```

Notice that this is an unnamed function that is immediately invoked. This is a common pattern with goroutines, but also notice that we defined the function as taking a single parameter (the url). The reason this function doesn't reference the url directly —which it is allowed to do—is that the rules of closure are such that if we did that, all four goroutines would probably end up seeing the same value for url. This is because url is changed by the for loop.

Finally, at the end of our program, we loop four times to pull the four results off of the channel, compare that results to the current biggest, and swap if it's bigger:

```
var biggest HomePageSize

for range urls {
    result := <-results
    if result.Size > biggest.Size {
        biggest = result
    }
}
```

Exercises

1. How do you specify the direction of a channel type?
2. Write your own `Sleep` function using `time.After`.
3. What is a buffered channel? How would you create one with a capacity of 20?

CHAPTER 11

Next Steps

You now have all the information necessary to write most Go programs. However, there are still some nuances and advanced techniques you must learn—programming is as much a craft as it is just having knowledge. This chapter will provide you with some suggestions about how best to master the craft of programming.

Study the Masters

Part of becoming a good artist or writer is studying the works of the masters. It's no different with programming. One of the best ways to become a skilled programmer is to study the source code produced by others. Go is well suited to this task because the source code for the entire project is freely available.

For example, we might take a look at the source code to the io/ioutil library available at *golang.org/src/pkg/io/ioutil/ioutil.go*.

Read the code slowly and deliberately. Try to understand every line and take a look at the supplied comments. For example, in the ReadFile method, there's a comment that says this:

```
// It's a good but not certain bet that FileInfo
// will tell us exactly how much to read, so
// let's try it but be prepared for the answer
// to be wrong.
```

This method probably started out simpler than what it became, so this is a great example of how programs can evolve after testing and why it's important to supply comments with those changes. The source code for all of the packages is available at *golang.org/src/pkg/*.

Make Something

One of the best ways to hone your skills is to practice coding. There are a lot of ways to do this—you could work on challenging programming problems from sites like Project Euler (*http://projecteuler.net/*), or try your hand at a larger project. Perhaps try to implement a web server or write a simple game.

Team Up

Most real-world software projects are created by teams, so learning how to work on a team is crucial. If you can, find a friend or a classmate and team up on a project. Learn how to divide a project into pieces you can both work on simultaneously.

Another option is to work on an open source project. Find a third-party library, write some code (perhaps fix a bug), and submit it to the maintainer. Go has a growing community that can be reached via the mailing list (*http://groups.google.com/group/golang-nuts*).

Answers

Chapter 1

1. Whitespace is the space between characters made up of space, tab, and newline characters.

2. A comment is a section of code ignored by the compiler that can be used as a note for anyone reading the code. The two types of comments are // (which goes to the end of the line) and /* */.

3. The files in the fmt package would begin with package fmt.

4. In order to use the Exit function from the os package, you would need to import the os package: import "os" and then invoke it with .: os.Exit().

5. Modifying the program to print with your name:

```go
package main

import "fmt"

func main() {
    fmt.Println("Hello, my name is Caleb")
}
```

Chapter 2

1. Integers are stored on a computer by using a base-2, binary number system.

2. The largest eight-digit number in binary is 255.

3. Program that computes $32{,}132 \times 42{,}452$ and prints it to terminal:

```
package main

import "fmt"

func main() {
    fmt.Println(32132 * 42452)
}
```

4. A string is a sequence of characters. You can find the length of a string using the len function (`len("a string")`).

5. The value of the expression is `true`.

Chapter 3

1. Two ways to create a new variable are: `var x = 5` or `x := 5`.

2. The value of x after running the equation is 6.

3. Scope is the range of places a variable can be used. Scope in Go is determined lexically using blocks, so look for the nearest curly braces.

4. Unlike a variable, the value of a constant is determined at compile time and cannot change throughout the lifetime of a program.

5. Program that converts Fahrenheit to Celsius:

```
package main

import "fmt"

func main() {
    fmt.Print("Enter a number: ")
    var input float64
    fmt.Scanf("%f", &input)

    output := (input - 32) * 5/9

    fmt.Println(output)
}
```

6. Program that converts feet into meters:

```go
package main

import "fmt"

func main() {
    fmt.Print("Enter a number: ")
    var input float64
    fmt.Scanf("%f", &input)

    output := input * 0.3048

    fmt.Println(output)
}
```

Chapter 4

1. The program prints: Small.
2. Program that prints out all numbers between 1 and 100 that are divisible by 3:

```go
package main

import "fmt"

func main() {
    for i := 1; i <= 100; i++ {
        if i % 3 == 0 {
            fmt.Println(i)
        }
    }
}
```

3. Program that prints numbers 1 through 100, but replaces multiples of 3 with "Fizz," multiples of 5 with "Buzz," and multiples of both 3 and 5 with "FizzBuzz":

```go
package main

import "fmt"

func main() {
    for i := 1; i <= 100; i++ {
        if i%3 == 0 && i%5 == 0 {
            fmt.Println("FizzBuzz")
        } else if i%3 == 0 {
            fmt.Println("Fizz")
        } else if i%5 == 0 {
            fmt.Println("Buzz")
        } else {
            fmt.Println(i)
        }
    }
}
```

Chapter 5

1. You access the fourth element of an array or slice with: `arr[3]`.

2. The length of the slice is 3.

3. The array would give you: `[c d e]`.

4. Program that finds the smallest number in the list:

```go
package main

import "fmt"

func main() {
    var min int
    x := []int{
        48, 96, 86, 68,
        57, 82, 63, 70,
        37, 34, 83, 27,
        19, 97, 9, 17,
    }
    for i, v := range x {
        if i == 0 || v < min {
            min = v
        }
    }
}
```

```
        fmt.Println(min)
    }
```

Chapter 6

1. The sum function signature in Go looks like: func sum(xs []int) int.

2. Function that halves an integer and returns true if even value or false if odd value:

```
func half(x int) (int, bool) {
    return x/2, x%2==0
}
```

3. Function with a variadic parameter that finds the greatest number in a list of numbers:

```
func max(xs ...int) int {
    var max int
    for i, x := range xs {
        if i == 0 || x > max {
            max = x
        }
    }
    return max
}
```

4. makeOddGenerator function that generates odd numbers:

```
func makeOddGenerator() func() uint {
    i := uint(1)
    return func() (ret uint) {
        ret = i
        i += 2
        return
    }
}
```

5. Recursive function that can find fib(n):

```
func fibonacci(n int) int {
    switch n {
    case 0:
        return 0
    case 1:
        return 1
    default:
        return fibonacci(n-1) + fibonacci(n-2)
    }
}
```

6. `Defer` defers a function to the moment before the surrounding function returns. `Panic` causes the function to immediately terminate along with any calling function and ultimately, the program itself. `Recover` is a way to prevent panics from going any further up the stack of functions. You can recover from a `panic` by deferring a call to a function which then calls the builtin `recover` function:

```
func f() {
    defer func() {
        if x := recover(); x != nil {
            fmt.Println("RECOVERED:", x)
        }
    }()
    panic("panic!")
}
```

7. To get the memory address of a variable, use the & operator: `y = &x`.

8. To assign a value to a pointer, use the * operator: `*x = 5`.

9. To create a pointer, use the `new` function: `x = new(int)`.

10. The value of `x` is 2.25.

11. Program to swap two integers:

```
func swap(x, y *int) {
    *x, *y = *y, *x
}
```

Chapter 7

1. The difference between a method and a function is that a method has a receiver while a function does not.

2. You would use an embedded anonymous field instead of a normal named field in order to use methods directly on the containing type.

3. Adding a new `perimeter` method to the `Shape` interface to calculate the perimeter of a shape, and implementing the method for `Circle` and `Rectangle`:

```
type Shape interface {
    perimeter() float64
}

func (c *Circle) perimeter() float64 {
    return 2 * math.Pi * c.r
}

func (r *Rectangle) perimeter() float64 {
    l := distance(r.x1, r.y1, r.x1, r.y2)
    w := distance(r.x1, r.y1, r.x2, r.y1)
```

```
        return 2 * (l + w)
    }
```

Chapter 8

1. Packages are a good software engineering practice. They allow us to break up large programs into smaller, easier to understand, and easier to maintain programs. They also encourage software reuse.

2. Identifiers that start with a capital letter are exported (meaning accessible from other packages), whereas identifiers that start with a lowercase letter are not.

3. A package alias is an alternative name for a package that you can specify when you import the package: import f "fmt".

4. Min and Max functions that find the minimum and maximum values in a slice of float64s:

```
    func Max(xs []float64) float64 {
        var max float64
        for i, x := range xs {
            if i == 0 || x > max {
                max = x
            }
        }
        return max
    }

    func Min(xs []float64) float64 {
        var min float64
        for i, x := range xs {
            if i == 0 || x < min {
                    min = x
            }
        }
        return min
    }
```

5. To document the functions created in #4, add comments before the functions. Those comments will show up as documentation for the godoc tool.

Chapter 9

1. NaN is returned for an empty list. Function modified to return 0:

```go
func Average(xs []float64) float64 {
    if len(xs) == 0 {
        return 0
    }
    total := float64(0)
    for _, x := range xs {
        total += x
    }
    return total / float64(len(xs))
}
```

2. Series of tests for the Min and Max functions written in the previous chapter:

```go
package math

import "testing"

func TestMath(t *testing.T) {
    cases := []struct {
        xs       []float64
        max, min float64
    }{
        {
            xs:  []float64{3, 5, 2, 1, 7, 9},
            max: 9,
            min: 1,
        },
        {
            xs:  []float64{},
            max: 0,
            min: 0,
        },
    }

    for _, c := range cases {
        max := Max(c.xs)
        if max != c.max {
            t.Errorf("expected %f got %f", c.max, max)
        }
        min := Min(c.xs)
        if min != c.min {
            t.Errorf("expected %f got %f", c.min, min)
        }
```

```
        }
    }
```

Chapter 10

1. You specify the direction of a channel type by using `<-`: `<-chan int` for receive-only channels or `chan<- int` for send-only channels.

2. `Sleep` function using `time.After`:

   ```
   func Sleep(duration time.Duration) {
       <-time.After(duration)
   }
   ```

3. A buffered channel allows send operations to succeed regardless of whether or not there is a receiver on the other end by storing the sent message in a buffer. To create a buffered channel, specify a buffer size as an argument to make: `make(chan int, 20)`.

Index

About the Author

Caleb Doxsey is a New York City–based developer who enjoys helping new programmers learn Go. He works as a software engineer at DataDog, building monitoring software for the cloud.

Colophon

The animal on the cover of *Introducing Go* is a Botta's pocket gopher (*Thomomys bottae*). It is part of the Geomyidae family and can be found in western North America. They are also known as valley pocket gophers.

In terms of size, the Botta's pocket gopher is considered medium in comparison with other gopher breeds. Males are typically larger than females, weighing between 5.6–8.8 ounces, and 4.2–7.1 ounces, respectively. Length varies between 6–10 inches from the tip of the nose to the end of the tail. Colors of this particular gopher range from a light gray to black and usually depend on the color of the soil in which a particular gopher inhabits. Gophers of darker skin tones and ones that suffer from albinoism have also been spotted. The "pocket" in their name is derived from the two pouches found at their cheeks and extending to their shoulders.

Botta's pocket gophers are strictly herbivores and their water consumption comes from eating a variety of vegetation. They pull plants underground from their roots and typically eat within their burrows. They are able to do this using their two front teeth, which are located outside of the mouth. They will eat for most of their waking hours, but those hours are not limited to day or night times. They have been known to forage above ground at night with the safety of darkness.

Breeding for the Botta's pocket gopher typically takes place during the spring months, though in areas with plenty of food resources, it can happen year round. Being solitary animals with one adult to each burrow, males will go in search of females. This usually happens more than once during breeding season, as females outnumber males in the population. Gestation is a short 18–19 days. Litters can be as large as 12 hairless and blind pups, but are usually much smaller in size (typically 1–7). Pups will start to wean and become independent around 40 days after birth.

Many of the animals on O'Reilly covers are endangered; all of them are important to the world. To learn more about how you can help, go to *animals.oreilly.com*.

The cover image is from a loose plate, the source of which is unknown. The cover fonts are URW Typewriter and Guardian Sans. The text font is Adobe Minion Pro; the heading font is Adobe Myriad Condensed; and the code font is Dalton Maag's Ubuntu Mono.

Get even more for your money.

Join the O'Reilly Community, and register the O'Reilly books you own. It's free, and you'll get:

- $4.99 ebook upgrade offer
- 40% upgrade offer on O'Reilly print books
- Membership discounts on books and events
- Free lifetime updates to ebooks and videos
- Multiple ebook formats, DRM FREE
- Participation in the O'Reilly community
- Newsletters
- Account management
- 100% Satisfaction Guarantee

Signing up is easy:

1. Go to: oreilly.com/go/register
2. Create an O'Reilly login.
3. Provide your address.
4. Register your books.

Note: English-language books only

To order books online:
oreilly.com/store

For questions about products or an order:
orders@oreilly.com

To sign up to get topic-specific email announcements and/or news about upcoming books, conferences, special offers, and new technologies:
elists@oreilly.com

For technical questions about book content:
booktech@oreilly.com

To submit new book proposals to our editors:
proposals@oreilly.com

O'Reilly books are available in multiple DRM-free ebook formats. For more information:
oreilly.com/ebooks

Lightning Source UK Ltd.
Milton Keynes UK
UKOW05f1527120616

276039UK00004B/11/P